Far too many people to
who you are, I thank y(
heart.

Edited by Sue Wilby.

Cover and layout artwork by Creeds of Bridport.
www.creedsuk.com
Cover design Chris Kirtley.
Cover photo Frank Kirtley.

Printed March 2020.

All rights reserved Chris Kirtley.
chriskirtley@yahoo.ie

The Duelling Pianist

Chris Kirtley

Chapter 1

Rick slammed his hand down on the keyboard as hard as he could. Thumb on G, two octaves below middle C, and his little finger, complete with skull ring, on the G an octave below. Twenty thousand watts of Crown amplifiers did their job, and the JBL speakers exploded into life. The crowd went wild.

Rick left it hanging in the air, as the anticipation grew to bursting point. They knew what was coming, I knew what was coming and Rick was a master at 'reading the room', this is a term we musicians use as an instinctive way of feeling when to lift the tempo, volume, mood or slip back a little to get underneath them and lift the atmosphere, or to take a break completely and start again. It's a science you pick up with experience of playing gigs to insane fans or empty rooms. Rick and I had a telepathy built over the years of playing together. He didn't even have to look at me. The octave hung over the crowd who were chanting "Now! Now! Now!"

I instinctively knew when he was going to go for it. The drummer didn't. Rick gave him a nod, no counting, nothing, just raised his hand again and similar to a musical conductor who lifts his baton on the upbeat and drops it on beat one of the first bar, he slammed it down again. We were off! "Great balls of fire" at 100 miles an hour or, depending on how much Rick had shoved up his nose, it could be even quicker.

It was never slower.

The crowd leapt into a jive. The JBL's screamed and vibrated every glass, every bottle, and sinew in the bar. You'd have to be nailed to the floor not to move to this. Rick was a master entertainer, a brilliant pianist, studied at Goldsmiths University but was thrown out after destroying half a dozen pianos. Once he stuck drawing pins into every hammer on a piano, to turn it into a harpsichord, and after several complaints from others in "soundproof" rehearsal rooms, who said they couldn't hear their Bach or Schubert, or whatever it was they were studying, because of Rick's volume.

Tonight felt good. The crowd were well oiled. The DJ had done his job and warmed them up to near boiling point. We were the "Duelling Pianos", imported from the US where it was known as "Crazy Pianos" but we couldn't use that name due to copyright. Complete with a bass player and a drummer it was the two on pianos who were the focus of the crowd. We would leap and jump and in Rick's case contort himself at, on, and sometimes, in the piano. We would try to outplay each other. We would take a song each and build the evening to a climax, throw in a 'last waltz' power ballad, and then send them home happy, hopefully. How we were going to build on this start beat me. Great Balls was thundering along. Rick screaming out the vocals like a demented banshee. No saving the voice, no easing into it. Straight in - in his inevitable way of "Do as much as you can for as long as you can." The drummer gave me a look and puffed out his cheeks as if to say "Crickey". Ray was a great drummer, a giant and sat over his kit making it look like a toy from Woolies, but he came down on the beat like a well-oiled clock. Sometimes just before the beat to give it a 'push,' and others, behind the beat, to relax the feel, but miss one? Never.

Paul on bass was equally in time, locked into Ray's drumming, tight as a dovetail joint.

(Rick thought that was a drug he hadn't tried yet.)

The four of us were now motoring like a steam train at full chat. We were well into the song now, and it was time for us to show off a little. Rick yelled, "Take it Chris" my cue to take a lead break and try to dazzle the crowd with some tasty licks on piano. I played by ear, never got past grade 5 but could hold my own on a pub piano and keep people in the bar, rather than chase them out. I came in bang on time, I knew this because Rick threw me a knowing nod. Top end of the piano where I was most comfortable, my left hand was crap. I hammered out 16s, (16 stabs per bar) which I had managed to make sound like a road drill - my dad always told me to stop knocking the end off the bloody piano. We would do lots of musical Q&As, Rick would play eight bars lead, I would play eight bars lead, and we would alternate trying to outdo each other every turn. I finished my first break, the audience showing approval. Usually we'd go into the next verse, but Rick had other ideas. Straight into his lead as if to say, "This is how it's done". He took the crowd with him, they were leaping, jiving, and throwing beer into the air. Rick looked at me, I started my second answer to his question trying to find an extra note or two, to keep up.

Ray puffed, and pulled the snare drum closer to him and whacked it even harder, speeding up ever so slightly for effect. Paul instinctively knew what was needed and went with him naturally. It was great to work with these two guys. I've never met two musicians that I haven't had to say what I would like them to do. They just did it, and ever so well.

I reckoned Great Balls, was now topping 110 mph but we never, ever lost it. The big crescendo ending after solos and assaulting the piano mercilessly (in Rick's case) was as tight as you could get it.

Rick did a final leap into the air and came down bang on time. A nanosecond of silence before the crowd went crazy. There was such a buzz in the room. Without any delay I started the next song. Ray puffed again. I screamed "1 2 3 4" and went into "She was just Seventeen", we all knew the set off by heart. Forty-five minutes of pure rock 'n' roll, no slow ones, no let up, just relentless hammering; maybe a ballad at the end so the crowd could smooch, and the guys could get up close to someone they've been eyeing all night. The floor was visibly bending as the crowd jumped in time. Rick did his stuff, I did mine, and sometimes we would end up on the same piano pretending to fight. The evening rose to its usual climax. We finished with "I'm down" the Beatles number Rick loved, as he was often down, fighting depression, and he reckoned this song brought him out of it. His vocals easily matched McCartney's. I felt proud of him. We left the stage to tumultuous noise. We could hear, "We want more," "We want more," from the dressing room.

"Well?" I said.

"Yeah," said Rick, "let's give 'em 'Great balls' again."

Ray puffed, and we were off at 120 mph.

The manager came backstage and paid us.

"Bloody great!" He enthused.

"Good take?" I asked

"Yeah!" He beamed, "Four grand, plus the door. I reckoned over 500 in there at a tenner a pop, not too bad at all."

I paid Ray and Paul. Ray puffed and put it in his back pocket. The rest I split with Rick who never counted it, checked it, or doubted me, just stuck it into his pocket with his usual "Thanks man".

I would have done this job for nothing. I loved it so much, but nothing beats that feeling of sticking a nice wedge of notes away at the end of a great night.

"Come on, and I'll drop you home." I said.

Rick didn't drive, a good job as he was rarely sober or sane enough. He always looked dirty in a sexy way; girls were all over him. I never got a look in being the 'straighter' of the duo. Ray and Paul left saying see you tomorrow. We were just up the road in a Whitbread venue. I loved local gigs as I could get home to Yvonne, my wife, and Ed, our eight-year-old.

"Take me to the Lion?" Rick asked. An all-nighter where all sorts of debauchery went on. Rick was addicted to any substance he could get hold of, women, sex, and his music of course.

"Oh come on," I said, "haven't you had enough?"

"It's only two." Rick indicated to his watch.

"Ok, come on then, I'm whacked and make sure you're okay for tomorrow night."

"Sure man!"

Don't know why I said that, he was always 'Ok' for tomorrow night, a true professional. He could party all night, all the next day, and still be an insane live wire at the piano, and go on partying more, like there was no tomorrow.

I closed the door behind me. Oh, that lovely smell of washing drying. A small table lamp had been left on for me. In the fridge I found a leftover dinner plated up with a note saying,

"Don't be too long darling xx"

another in crayon said,

"I helped make this dad!" :)

I wolfed the lot down, turned off the lamp and tried to miss the stairs that creaked.
Ed was fast asleep, making little chortling noises. He was obviously happy in dreamland, probably driving a fire engine and catching people as they jumped from buildings. He loved the idea of someone holding a blanket tightly and people escaping by jumping into it.

"Funny if they bounce back into the building!!" He once said and squealed with delight at his own humour. I tucked him in and kissed him gently and I'm sure he smiled. I sneaked in next to Yvonne trying not to disturb her. She instinctively turned her back to me and stuck out her rear, we fitted perfectly like a jigsaw. I slid an arm under her neck and the other one over her and pulled her gently into me. She didn't change her breathing and I fell into a deep sleep with the smell of a very comforting baby shampoo.

Somewhere, not so far away, I was sure I could hear Rick playing some Tom Waits in a smoky, stinking, sticky bar with the three girls he had squeezed into the van when I gave him a lift. Surely, he wasn't that loud.

Was he?

At this time of night? …

Chapter 2

Rick was my best friend. We met a couple of years earlier, in "The Sir Richard Steele." A pub on Haverstock Hill NW3, a posh part of North London. Sir Richard Steele was a dramatist, a writer, so the pub attracted lots of actors and musicians and artists alike. I loved that pub. I would drink with the likes of Tony Ashton, from Ashton, Gardner, and Dyke who had a devilish sense of humour. An amazing Hammond organ player, who penned "The Resurrection Shuffle", one of their megahits. One night he joined in with some terrified carol singers, collecting for charity singing, or shouting, silent night at full belt with his rough, well overused and punished voice. Eric Burdon bought me a pint there. Robert Powell drank there with his wife Babs, from Pans People. Twiggy gave me a smile once and on one notable night "Judd" a P.R. guy on the same label as Abba, and who played harmonica on Boy George's "Chameleon", locked himself in the ladies with a set of bagpipes and wouldn't come out. I never knew bagpipes could sound so loud. It was very funny.

Rick and I hit it off straight away. He was in The Steeles one night trying to play the piano. He was out of his tree and the locals kept dragging him off it. He did look like a feral kid off the street. Things got violent and he got thrown out. I heard something in what he had managed to play, intriguing, so I followed him out and shouted, "Hey! Hang on a minute."

"What the fuck do you want?" He snarled at me.

"Whoa Whoa, hang on." I said it with my arms out, trying to stop him coming at me.

"Got any stuff?" He asked.

"No." l replied.

"Fuck off then."

"Let's go over the road to the Haverstock Arms and I'll buy you whatever you want."

"What do you want?" Rick snarled.

"Come on." l said, "I liked your playing and want to chat to you about an idea I have."

"They got keys over there?"

"A piano? No sorry, it's quiet."

"Fuck that. l don't do quiet."

"Chris." I said holding out my hand.

"Rick." He said, and just walked out into the road towards the pub. How that black cab missed him, I'll never know.

"God it's fucking dull in here." He said, not quietly.

"What you having?" I asked.

"J.D. and Coke," he replied, looking around like a tourist in New York. "Please." he added.

"Go grab a seat." I pointed to a less busy spot.
I handed him his drink and I sat down, when I looked up at him, his glass was empty.

"I knew I should have said a double". He complained.

"That WAS a double." I said.
I went and bought him another one, this one lasted a tad longer.

"So, what do you wanna talk about?" He asked, looking around me like I had an aura, or something I didn't know draped over my head.

"I've been toying with this idea about two pianos on stage. It's not original. They do it in the States, but no one is doing it here"

"And how would that work?" He sniffed loudly.

"Simple, two pianos, twice the fun, twice the energy a kind of buy one get one free, for the audience."

"Hmmmm." Then after a long pause staring into his bubbling Coke mesmerized almost, by the colours, the ice, and those bubbles, "How good are you?" His eyes tracing my head and shoulders now.

"Dunno, reckon I can do it. I've played in the Firkin pubs for years now. Lived off the tips. Two of us on stage could raise a little mayhem."

"Oh I can do mayhem." said Rick, breaking out into a wicked smile.

"Why don't I book Tooley Street (A dark, under the railway arches rehearsal room, used by every band in town.) I can get two pianos and a P.A. down there. Gary

Clarke, who's involved with Rank is interested. They have a venue in a new multiplex in Hemel (Hempstead) and don't know what to do with it. When I put the idea to him, he jumped at it."

"Ok, why not?" He seemed genuinely interested. I was expecting a "No thanks, but I'll have another JD and Coke please."

He had another JD and Coke, and another, and another, he drank them like I drank pints. We talked about influences and had a surprisingly amount in common. Dr. John, Waits (Tom), Oscar Peterson, Jacques Lousier, Dudley Moore,

"Dudley Moore?" Rick almost choked on his drink. "Dudley fucking Moore?"

"Keep your voice down." I said.

"He's a comedian!" Rick said, face in disbelief.

"I know! And a brilliant jazz pianist too, listen to 'Sooz Blooz." I enthused.

"Think he was shagging her?" Asked Rick.

"Who?"

"Sue!"

"No! It's spelt with a Z," I said.

"Zooz Blooze?"

"NO! Just give it a listen, you'll love it."

Only then I discovered his sense of humour, as a wry smile came over his face. He was playing me all along. He knew the track.

Rick turned up bang on time at Tooley Street, with whom I was later to discover was his long-suffering girlfriend Sonja. She would hang on every word, every arm, and Rick always looked like he didn't give a toss, but he loved her deeply. She kept him grounded. Stopped him going off on one, and still Rick's addiction to other women didn't put her off, or didn't seem to. She just kicked his arse every time she found him with someone or if he didn't come home. His arse must have been kicked a hell of a lot.

"Gary, this is Rick. Rick, Gary." Rick shook Gary's hand. I remembered being a bit miffed that he hadn't shook mine back at the Steeles.

"Son." Rick said introducing his 'bird' as he always referred to her as. Affectionately though, I'm sure.

"Oi!" Said Rick, studying the two grand piano shells with two Roland electric pianos inserted where the original keyboard would have been. They were wired up to 2 Marshall Stacks with a sub bass woofer under each piano.

"Oh, I like loud." He said taking off his jacket, and fiddling with the knobs on the Marshall amp.

I liked the way he set the EQ, he knew what he wanted, plenty of top, and plenty of bass. A quick flick of the Roland's controls and a very nice jazzy lick came thundering out of the Marshals.

"Well if you can keep up with me, I'll think about it."

At that point he went into a walking bass with his left hand, and counterpart syncopated chords with his right. I knew immediately it was a "Whole Lotta Shaking" by

Jerry Lee Lewis. I jumped onto the other piano and matched him note for note. This had a phasing effect, as you never get the two parts exactly on time together. I felt a tremendous shake go through my body, like someone had just walked over my grave, only this was at Marshall number 11 volume. I didn't even notice the trains going overhead. God this was going to be good, great, and then Rick started to sing. I thought nothing could get over the din we were making, but his voice cut through like a siren, at Marshall number 11 volume.

We hadn't even discussed what material we would do, but for half an hour Rick went through song after song, mainly Jerry Lee Lewis stuff, giving me a nod when he wanted me to take a solo. In a split-second gap, I started playing, "She was just Seventeen" he was straight there beating the shit out of the piano, but oh, so beautifully. Backing me this time, not trying to steal it at all. This was going to work, and this was going to be bonkers. Gary was grinning from wall-to-wall and kept giving me the thumbs up. When we stopped, I looked at Rick and said, "Wow! We haven't even rehearsed anything yet!"

"I don't do rehearse." He came back with immediately. "When do we start?"

It wasn't a question.

Chapter 3

Ed dived onto the bed.
"Dad! Dad! How'd it go?"
"Hiya buddy!" I pulled him in next to me.
"Nee Naw Nee Naw!!"
"No not that, last night I mean!" Ed knew I was teasing him. He just loved anything to do with fire engines.
"It was crazy. Rick was his usual."
Rick and Ed got on like a house on fire. When he came around to go to a gig, he'd pick Ed up and throw him in the air, and for a heart stopping moment I prayed he would catch him. He always did.
"Don't let Yvonne see you do that." I would say, but Rick would just laugh and wink at Ed.
"Hi babe". Yvonne appeared with a cup of coffee. I always liked a coffee in bed to start my day, and the three of us would sit and chat about lovely nonsense, and far-off dreams of holidays, and shopping, and more chitchat about superfluous stuff, which seemed so important and serious, especially to Ed.
"Where are you tonight again? I forgot." Yvonne asked.
"Just up the road, so I'll be home later."

"Great," she said, "I hate it when you have to stay over."

Rick and I often shared a room to save money, but I hardly saw him. He'd roll up at nine or ten in the morning and crash. At least I got a good night's worth. If he did come back, he was often never alone, and I would dive under the covers and try to sleep. God knows what he was doing with them. I'd never heard girls make noises like that before.

"Can you collect Ed from school? I'm meeting mum for shopping."

"Sure." I said. "We'll have a "purple moment" in the van." This involved Deep Purple at full chat as we drove away from the school. Ed thought it was really cool.

"YAY!" shrieked Ed.

"Come on Tiger, let's get you to school and let Daddy sleep a bit more."

Yvonne and I had a wonderful relationship. She knew when to leave me to sleep and when to kick my arse out of bed. When to make love, and when to play cool. When to disturb me, and when not to. She gave me a kiss on my lips, said have a good day, and don't forget Ed.

As if I would.

Gary rang and said they were rolling out another venue. Hemel had been a great success. Would Rick and I do the opening, and could we find a couple of deps for Hemel? If they cut the mustard it would be a permanent job for them, alternating between Hemel and Brighton.

"Brighton?"

"Yep that's the new venue. An old cinema, Rank closed years ago and they want to bring it back to life as Duelling Pianos."

"When?" I asked.

"Oct the 5th in four weeks. Is that enough time to get another two guys on track?"

"Argh, it's my birthday on the seventh." I said. "Can't the new guys do Brighton, so at least I can be home that weekend? We have a birthday breakfast it's a very special treat for all of us."

We had a long-standing tradition of a very special birthday breakfast treat. We would do it for each other, a decadent mix of pancakes, bacon, maple syrup, freshly squeezed orange juice, fresh ground coffee, and lots of sweet sticky hugs and other delights.

"No, sorry you two must do the opening few weekends, to get it going. They're looking for another Hemel success."

"Ok, suppose so. Have you talked to them about more dough? I'd like to give Ray and Paul a bit more, they're priceless."

"See what I can do." Gary said, unconvincingly.

Big corporates never wanted to spend anything.

Rather make the place look good with cheap artefacts, and poor deco. They pay their staff peanuts and they even want the shells back.

"See you in the office before you start tonight?" Asked Gary.

"Yeah sure thing."

"Rick okay?" Gary was always worried Rick wouldn't show, or get arrested, or overdose.

"Yeah fine. Rick will always be okay." I assured him.

"Great, catch you later then. Bye."

"See you".

I hung up the phone and it immediately rang.

Rick had been arrested.

"What's he done now?" I asked Sonja, who was panicking and hyperventilating on the other end of the phone.

"He - broke - into - my - stepmother's - house." She said with a deep breath between every word.

"Calm down, breathe slower,.. That's better."

Sonja took a big breath in and in one sentence said,

"He broke into my stepmother's house, to steal back the cat that she stole from dad to get at him, when I told Rick he just marched around there, kicked the door in, found the cat under the bed, called her a bitch, and nearly kicked her head in, but managed to pull it, left her screaming hysterically, marched out with the cat and handed him to me, and screamed, "BITCH" again as we left. I don't know what to do. The next thing we knew two police officers were at our door arresting him on aggravated burglary and__"

"Son. Son!" I said, trying to calm her down.

"Where are you now?"

"Hampstead nick." She said, sounding relieved she had found me on the other end of the phone. I was always calming them down before, during, and after violent, verbal rows. Sonja had abandonment issues, after being the one her mother gave away because she couldn't afford the upkeep of two children. She had missed her identical twin painfully ever since that fateful day. She trusted me to look after Rick. She told me he was a different person after we had met, that he had found a purpose in life, an outlet for his genius playing and extrovert personality, a platform on which he could show off, and he loved the fact that at last people loved him, he wallowed in the adoration. When he was on stage, he was a king. He felt useful for once.

"I'll be right there, sit tight. Was he carrying anything?"

"No. We were on the sofa just relaxing with a drink. Rick was resting, nothing on him."

Well that was a relief, I thought, at least he won't get banged up for possession.

"Ok, on my way. Tell Rick I'm coming and to stay calm."

"Ok, thanks Chris." She hung up.

Shit, I thought, jumping out of bed, throwing last night's clothes on and diving out into the van.

"Oh, thank God." Sonja threw herself into my arms.

"Thanks, thanks for coming. They won't let me see him."

"Ok, let's go and find him."
Sonja held onto my arm, and I could feel she was shaking quite violently.

"Hi, come to see Rick". I said to the desk sergeant, "and get him out hopefully".

"Who?" asked the desk sergeant.

"Oh, I mean Richard Morelidge, sorry". I added.

"Who are you?" He asked.

"Chris, his best friend, I've come to get him out." I said again.

"Not sure that's gonna happen." He grunted, not even looking up.

"Why? What's he done?" I asked.

"Violent entry, threatening behavior, theft."

"Theft? What did he steal?"

"A cat."

"A cat? It was HER cat!" I said pointing to Sonja, who was nodding frantically, as if to confirm what I was saying was the whole truth and so on.

"Your cat?" He asked Son.

"Yes!" She blurted, "he's a male neutered tabby called Ziggy, with a bit of his tail missing and different sized ears and he's__"

"Alright, alright!" Barked the desk sergeant. "You'll have to get Mrs. Anderson__"

"That's my step mum." Sonja said. "She stole Ziggy from my dad, and Rick went to get him back, he wasn't stealing him; he's mine, he's__"

"ALRIGHT!" Barked the desk sergeant again. "You'll have to get Ms. Anderson to come down and make a statement, and drop the charges, otherwise he's staying put."

"Ok." I said. We'll go and get her. Can I see Rick now please?"

"Who?" The sergeant asked being deliberately awkward.

"Never mind," and I left with Sonja hanging onto my arm, still shaking.

"Where is she?"

"Probably at home." Son said.

"Let's go and get her. I've got to get Rick out of here before tonight, or before he kicks off, whichever is the sooner. I was sure the desk sergeant would've loved that. He could be all powerful and lock him up for longer. Rick never gave a good first impression and I'm sure the sergeant would have loved to keep him in for as long as possible."

Mary Anderson lives on the estate, just around the corner from Sonja and her dad, she kicked him out after his drinking became intolerable. Since then he hadn't touched a drop. Mary didn't know that and, therefore, wouldn't have him back. I always thought she would have softened a little if she knew George had given up the drink, but George was so, so stubborn, and he didn't want her back anyway.

The door was being repaired as we approached.

"Hi" I said to one of the workmen.

"Is Mary in?"

"Think so." He said, beckoning me to enter.

"Mary?" I shouted.

"Mary!" I shouted again. "M……"

"What?" She sounded so grumpy and looked even grumpier.

"Mary, can we sort this? Rick's locked up and I need him out, and now."

"GOOD!" She snarled, pulling a contorted expression that I've never seen anyone pull before. "Where he deserves to be."

"Mum it's my cat." Pleaded Son.

"Oh, it's always Mum, when you want something isn't it Son? You spoilt little__"

"Mary stop it. It's not going to achieve anything is it? Rick would never hurt you; you know that. He was only trying to get Son's cat back for her. You did nick it in the first place."

"Yeah well that was to get at George, after what he did."

"Mary please!" I pleaded. "Do what you want to George, go round and sort him out, but it's Sonja's cat, and Rick is locked up, and I need him out, and out now."

"I don't have the bus fare." Mary was always looking for handouts.

At last, a glimmer of hope. She knew it was her fault really.

"I'll drive you down there, they just need you to drop the charges and they'll let Rick out."

"And bring me back?"

"Yes of course."

"Can we call into Tesco's on the way back?"

"Yes, yes, and I'll buy you whatever you want."

She disappeared inside, and seconds later came out with her coat on, and a newly applied bright red lipstick.

"Thanks." I said, "Thanks Mary."

"H," I said to the desk sergeant, "we've come to get Rick, sorry, er, Mr. Morelidge, and Mary here, is willing to drop all the charges. It was just a misunderstanding."

"Really?" He asked her, almost willing her to say, 'no not really.'

"Yes." she said, "He didn't mean it, and it's her cat anyway." Gesturing at Sonja, who nodded furiously again.

"So, it's criminal damage for him?" Nodding towards a corridor where the cells must be.

"And theft for you." He beamed at Mary.

"Oh for God's sakes!" I said.

"Careful lad, it'll be you next."

"What have I done?"

"Disrespecting a police officer."

I wondered if there was even a charge for that.

"Oh, come on". I protested, "think of the paperwork you won't have to do."

You sad bastard I thought, but managed to keep it in.

"Mary will sign wherever you want, and we'll all be on our way. No harm done."

"Bring out cell three." The sergeant shouted to no one in particular, but everyone on duty would have heard it. Some clanking of keys, and doors opening and slamming, and Rick appeared behind a rather tasty female officer, and I could see Rick was just focused on her rear.

"RICK!" I hissed loudly at him.

"Jesus, good to see you guys." He said, looking none the worse for his time inside.

"What the fuck are you doing here?" He shouted at Mary.

"Rick, not now I'm trying to get you out."

"OUT." shouted the sergeant not looking up once again.

"Hang on, I want her done for theft." Rick shouted. The desk sergeant looked up this time.

"Rick, come on."

I grabbed him firmly and marched him towards the door.

"Nothing to sign?" I asked, looking back at the sergeant.

"Nowt yet". He said, "Just get him out."
"Lock her up, the bitch." Rick was yelling.
Sonja kicked his arse, and Rick was out of the door.
"You take Rick home," I gave Sonja a twenty, "I'll take Mary back via Tesco's; you just make sure he's okay for tonight. Pick you up at six, Rick."
I knew he would be okay for tonight. Rick was always okay for tonight. "Come on. Tesco's."

"Hiya buddy."
"Hi dad, can we have Perfect Strangers on?"
Ed's new favourite purple song.
"Sure we can."
"And at number 11?" Ed asked.
"Of course. That's the only volume in the van." I winked.
Yvonne was already home, she could have easily picked Ed up, but knew we liked our 'boys time' together.
"Hi babe." She said. "Hi, big man," to Ed. "Good day?" Yvonne asked me.
"Well apart from Rick getting arrested for stealing a cat, yeah fine."
"What?"
"You just couldn't make it up." Tell you all later."
"Mum did you know Wendy Korking hasn't got a Willie?"
We both stifled a loud, snorting, snigger.

"Yeah! We were down in the bushes looking for slugs for Mrs. Bell. When me and Ian needed to pee, Wendy did one too, but she has no willy!!"

"Well…er, girls don't have one." She said, trying to be as calm and collected as she always is.

"Why?" Asked Ed, not seeming too bothered about it. I made a gesture to Yvonne, that I needed to make a phone call, and left them to it.

"Why?" Ed asked again and again.

It was all forgotten by dinner. The doorbell went at five and Ed raced to answer it. It was Rick and Sonja, ready for tonight's job. Sonja had made sure Rick was ready, by 'delivering' him to me. Rick went down on his knees and gave Ed a hug.

"Hi Yvonne." Sonja said. "Why don't you go tonight, and I'll stay in with Ed?" A really unselfish offer, as she didn't like Rick been out of her sight too often.

"No thanks, but that's very sweet of you." Yvonne said with one of her very loving smiles.

"You good?" I asked Rick.

"Yeah man. Thanks mate. Thanks for today, I tell you if I see her again, I'll__ "

"Stop!" I put my arm out, palm up to him. "Let it go, it's finished."

"Okay you're right."

"And I've got some news. Listen everyone."

Ed looked like he knew this was going to be serious.

"We've been asked to open Brighton in four weeks. It's a new venue for Rank, and they want us to open it."

"Great man." Rick nodded.

"Oh, that's good honey." Said Yvonne, "When?"

"October 7." I said, slightly cringing.

"But that's your birthday Sweetie." She protested.

"I know."

"But what about..," she paused looking at Rick and Sonja, "you know, our birthday 'thing'". Making quotation marks with her fingers.

Rick looked like a Labrador, who couldn't hear a high whistle, his head tilting to one side.

"Yeah Dad, your pancakes in bed!" Ed shouted.

"We can do that on another day, we'll make it special."

"Can't you get them to open the following week Dad?"

"Can't do that son, I'm not as important as them."

"Yes. You. Are." Ed said, hitting me on the leg as he said each word separately.

"Okay, great news really." Yvonne said, meaning it.

"Wow man, Brighton. Brilliant." Said Rick, excitedly, knowing it will be a hotel, and we will be sharing, and he could be manic for the weekend, without Son.

Sonja sighed, and shrugged her shoulders.

"Come on let's do it." Rick said.

I gave Yvonne a hug and a 'See you later.'

"Bye Ed, be a good boy, bed early."

"But it's Saturday tomorrow." He protested.

Rick and Sonja said their goodbyes.

"Come over Sunday." Yvonne said, "We're having Lamb."

"You bet!" Said Rick.

"Great!" Said Son.

"Urrrgghh!" Said Ed. "What do they do with the feaces?" He asked innocently.

"Feaces?" Rick asked, bewildered.

"Yeah," all that fluffy stuff on their backs."

"Fleeces!!" Yvonne said, and we all had a good laugh.

Rick slammed his hand down on the keyboard…

Chapter 4

Gary Clark was our agent. After years of playing piano in David Bruce's Firkin pubs, I decided to try the concept of two pianos on stage. Twice the mayhem I thought. Only problem was to find a venue big enough to get enough people in to afford two pianists. Gary was very supportive. He'd been sending me out on the Norwegian circuit for several years. A tight learning curve out there but very fulfilling for a musician.

The Scandinavians crave live music, and with zero alcohol tolerance during the week, they often don't drink at all on a 'school day'. Many of the bars only open Friday and Saturday night and boy, do the locals come out of the woodwork and pack a week's drinking into two nights. So, it was great for a musician, instant adoration and easy to get them crazy. Sometimes when Gary asked how a weekend went, I would answer, "Well the piano wasn't in the same place at the end of the night!" The punters would swing, and jive quite energetically, violently, often crashing into the piano and physically moving it a few inches. Or a few feet.
I spent many a night chasing it back and forth. I hated it at first. I didn't want to be away from Yvonne and Ed,

who'd just arrived in our life. I'll never forget my first job. It was in Bø, in Telemark, Norway. The address was simply 'Bø Versthuset' (pub) Bø Norge.

When I rang Gary for directions, he said the Norwegian agent he was working with had said just get off the bus in Bø and you will see it. I did. A single road in, and the same road out and one pub. A one-horse town, he'd said, and I'm sure the horse had left. The hospitality was truly amazing. Typical Norwegian friendliness.

"Welcome to Bø." Gunnar said, holding out his hand, and after a near bone crushing handshake, "Hungry?" He asked. "Biff and chips?"

"Yeah! Great!" I said, warming to the place already. The bar must have been over 100 years old. Solid walls, constructed of pine tree trunks. Whole stag heads on every wall, and the odd reindeer skin on the floor. The Norwegians hunted them for food and used the whole animal to feed on, keep warm, make moccasins, and make jewellry from the teeth and horn. Up in the far north the Sami were expert in this.

After a very generous steak and chips and coffee that furred up my teeth, I was shown where I would be playing. A large bar area with a grand piano shell housing a Yamaha electronic keyboard in place of the original. It had been nailed to the wall for effect, looking really cool.

"Great." I said, "I'll sound check if that's okay."

"Sure". Gunnar said. "Come and find me and I'll show you to your room." He said in perfect English.

"You start at 11."

I gave him a thumbs up. Normal working hours were usually 11pm to 3am, nobody came out before 11. The weekend went surprisingly well. They danced, jived, drank, fell over, fell over again, and eventually went home noisily.

Sunday morning over breakfast, which was bread with ham, cheese, sliced red pepper, juice, and that teeth furring coffee, Gunnar came to pay me, thanked me for a great weekend and asked me if I would come back?

"Yeah, sure." I said. "No!" I thought. It was too far away from my family. I felt helpless as I couldn't get back if anything, God forbid, happened.

"Where do I get the bus?" I asked.

"Right outside the door."

He pointed to a bus shelter; I didn't know was a bus shelter.

"Har du det bra, and tusen takk." (goodbye and thank you) he shouted, as I left.

The bus was due in about 20 minutes and with typical Norwegian efficiency it turned up, on the dot.

I put out my hand as the bus seemed to be not slowing, or indicating it was stopping. It went charging past, then with a hiss of airbrakes, and reversing back to the stop, the driver opened the door and yelled something at me.

"English please!" I said.

"What are you doing here?" He asked.

"Waiting for you, I think."

"Nobody gets on here." he said, beckoning me to get on. I was the only one on the bus. I sat right next to the driver, and he was delighted to have someone to show off his impeccable English to.

"That's the first time I have ever picked anyone up from there!"

Said a lot about the town I thought. He talked all the way back to the airport. I went back there several times, and Gunnar and I became great friends. He even came over with his wife, Irene, pronounced, 'I-ren-eh', but he hated our brown beer. After several years of backwards and forwards to Norway, I started getting tired of all the travelling. The gigs were great, but I wanted more time at home. I always earned my living playing piano somewhere, so I concentrated on finding work nearer home. After a few years in the Firkin pubs I was looking at the Duelling Pianos concept, and after meeting Rick on that fateful night in The Steeles, thought we could do it.

Rick was a loner; he was bumming around playing for tips and free beer. I could have found him work in the Firkin pubs, but he had no structure, no patience, Rick wasn't one for turning up regularly four nights a week, to play rugby songs to drunk, pretend rugby fans. Rick wanted to play, play from the soul, play dazzling solos, tasty boogie licks, he wanted to be listened to, he was very serious about his art and lived for the applause, the adoration, the women, and of course the alcohol. Rock and Roll was his bag and he could nail it every time. That night in the Steeles, he just wanted to play. The locals didn't want him to play, and out he went, you know the rest.

After the audition (something else Rick doesn't do) we went looking for suitable venues to try out the concept. Gary knew a lot of people in the trade, and we started out in some notable music pubs. 'The Golden Lion' in Fulham. 'The Mean Fiddler' in Willesden etc. It was just the two of us at first. One pianist would have to keep the rhythm going, a bit like a rhythm guitarist in a band only on piano this time, and the other sticking in melodic stabs and runs in between the vocals. This worked okay for a while, but it soon became apparent that a bass player and drummer would beef things up quite a bit, and also free us up to do some showman stuff and concentrate on trying to outplay each other. Which we did.

Gary had been talking with Craig Anders, manager of a new venue Top Rank were opening in Hemel Hempstead. A multiplex cinema, ice rink, swimming pool, complete with tubes going in and out of the building, a casino, several High Street fast food outlets, and an empty, massive theatre style area, which they didn't know what to do with. They had a hard-core nightclub on site, but wanted something quirky. Something new and different in this vast space.

Over several pints Gary had talked Craig into the idea of Duelling Pianos and managed, (Gary was good at managing), to get Craig along to one of our gigs. He couldn't have chosen a better night. Rick was on top form; I was playing catch up almost. Sometimes I let Rick go, he instinctively knew when to push the boundaries.

We were using old upright pianos then, with electric keyboards, shoehorned into where the original keyboard would have been. Rick was rocking his back and forth, using his knees as a fulcrum (we stood up and we played back-to-back) sometimes nearly losing it and having to pull the leaning piano back with his freehand. I actually thought of calling it 'Leaning Pianos', but that wouldn't have worked as I knew later, we would move onto grand pianos.

After two encores, and the manager frantically signaling us to stop, we were well over time, we ended the night with Rick's now traditional leap into the air and coming down bang on time, for the final big fat chord crescendo and sudden stop. The crowd went bananas, the lights came up, we were done.

At the bar, Gary came over with Craig, introduced him to us, and said, "Let's go for a curry, we need to talk."

Rick could eat for England or any other country for that matter, and we woofed back all sorts of Indian delights, it felt like a 'corporate do.'

"Have what you want and eat as much as you can." Gary said excitedly. "Expenses!" He winked.

We talked about the bar in Hemel. Craig wanted to know how it would work, what we needed, and how much it would cost etc. Rank always wanted to know how much it would cost. I said it would be much more visual, and effective if we could use two bright red grand piano shells, a bass player, and a drummer.

I could see Craig doing the maths, but he was well up for it. I could see him thinking he could take our idea, make some big money, and have a unique concept in the multiplex. He was very keen, said he would pitch it to the powers that be, and get back to us.

He got back to us within a couple of days and said he'd been told to get on with it, and make it happen quickly, the venue had to open soon.

We were drafted in as consultants, and for the first time in his life, Rick had a 'proper' job. Meetings after meetings with set designers, sound engineers, DJs, etc. The bar had been designed to replicate an old American distillery. Planks of wood over the walls. Copper stills, and masses of memorabilia nailed up everywhere.

I loved it.

The music we played would go down well here. It had the right ambience. Typically, Rank wanted to change it before we had played a note. They wanted the bar staff to dress hillbilly style, and do routines on stage between us, the DJ, and lookalike tribute acts.

"Oh no." I thought.

I managed to talk Craig into doing the lookalikes midweek to bring something different to the bar on weekdays and leave Friday and Saturday nights to us.

They left it to us.

We auditioned for a drummer and a bass player.
We found Ray, a rocksteady snare hitter, then Paul came along and we soon knew this was going to work. They fitted in as if they'd been there all along. No need for explaining how we worked, they instinctively knew and 'got it' first time.
We didn't rehearse much. Rick didn't rehearse at all, just sat at the side and listened with the occasional thumbs up. Once or twice jumping in and letting rip a bit, getting a little respect from the newcomers, I thought. We all agreed to 'wing it' on the night and have been 'winging it' ever since. It has always worked, some nights marvelously, some nights ballistically, never ordinary, and the energy had to be reined in sometimes, but we never lost it.

"Dad's on telly!" Shouted Ed.
The local 6.30 news covered the opening, as it was a massive multi-million-pound investment by Rank, and a great boost to the town's economy.

They queued around two sides of the building. It was Friday, and the locals were excited to see this new, shiny, dazzling building, open at last, and come to life.

The opening night was brilliant, a few glitches here and there, but we pulled off our part, and the following weeks were jammed every night. Rank were keen to roll out the whole concept nationwide, as they had plenty of empty cinemas. These would become Duelling Pianos on one level and a nightclub on the other level, normally the upstairs part. They also opened many newbuild sites with full blown multiplex everything. Rick and I opened Brighton, Southampton, Leeds, and Lincoln, to name a few.

They called the Duelling Piano bars 'Jumpin Jacks.'

Chapter 5

It was the week before the Brighton opening, all the work had been done. The sound was good, the lights were good. Rank were still busy organizing smoke machines, ice machines, security, staff, staff training, rehearsals, and so on. I was enjoying a well-earned night off. Yvonne was making a paella. She knew it was my favourite meal and she made a cracking seafood version. It always hit the spot. Comfort food at its best. It smelt gorgeous. I laid on the sofa with a glass of my favourite Grenache, and Ed appeared. He went to put a video in the VCR.

"What you up to Ed?" I asked, but already knew.

"I wanna watch Mega Machines." He said, his favourite fire engine video.

"But I'm just going to watch the news, you can watch that any time."

"Ok Dad, Then I'll watch it now."

How could I argue with that kind of logic? He wasn't being rude. Just took what I said literally. He took his whole life literally. Once we were looking at the sign for not leaving dog doo lying on the ground. Quite a graphic picture of a dog with a steaming deposit behind him, with a big red circle and a red cross through the centre of the said deposit, and a figure of a person kneeling down, behind the dog, scooping it up.

"What do you think that means?" I asked Ed.
Ed studied it for a while, his face at first frowning and then a big smile as he thought he'd got it.

"I know!" He said with a triumphant look, "it means, don't light fires behind dogs"!
How I managed to contain myself, I don't know.

"Not quite," I said, "but a good idea." Then I explained what it really meant. Ed was satisfied and off we both went, smiling.

Ed dived onto the sofa, I just managed to save my wine.

"Love you dad." He said, and hugged me tightly. We just got to the end of the video when Yvonne announced dinner was ready.

"Wash your hands Ed," came from the kitchen and he jumped up and ran off to the bathroom.
We loved mealtimes, a time of togetherness, catching up on lots of chatter. I was told off once by Yvonne for making them laugh so much, Ed nearly choked on his meatballs.

Rick, meanwhile, was having his own night off.

He and Sonja were at the 100 club in Oxford Street. Rick often went out with Sonja and went home with someone else. Sonja often leaving early due to work commitments. She was the receptionist at the local veterinary centre. Rick would stay and always be the last to be kicked out, often with someone on his arm. Sonja would rather be with him, than not be with him. Sex between them was always great. Sonja loved being handcuffed to the bed, and had four special pink furry handcuffs for the occasion. Once Rick handcuffed her to the bed and went out for the night. He swore to Sonja that he had forgotten he had handcuffed her to the bed, but then Rick carried on as if she had only been tied up for a few minutes.

Sonja had always said they had a flawed fascination for each other. I can't be with you, can't be without you situation. Right now, she couldn't be without Rick. Her father had separated, got together with Mary, it went catastrophically wrong as Mary had multiple personality disorder. I'm not even sure that existed, but Sonja's dad was sure of it. Rick was the only stable thing in Sonja's life. Not perfect but always there for her. Rick left the 100 club at 3am. He got home at 11am. Sonja was working, none the wiser, or head in the sand. To Sonja it didn't matter as Rick would be home when she got in after work, and all would be right in the world.

For the time being.

We left for Brighton on Thursday.

Thursday night would be a full-on rehearsal for staff members to make sure timings, and equipment all worked correctly. Top Rank managers, press and plus ones or plus twos would be invited to make up a crowd. Then they would run the night, and sort out any problems with a private audience. I said goodbye to Ed and Yvonne, made my apologies for not being home on my birthday, Sunday, and said I'd see them later in the day, for a get together of some sort.

I picked up Rick, who was saying goodbye to Sonja, who was lecturing Rick about behaving and not drinking too much. Fat lot of good that did.

"Hi mate." I said as Rick jumped into the van, blowing kisses to Sonja, who was still on the doorstep waving.

"Thank fuck for that." Said Rick, Sighing and settling down into the aircraft seats we'd had fitted.

"What's up?" I asked.

"Oh Son." Rick said, "she goes on sometimes, don't do this, don't do that."

"She only means well." I said.

"Yeah, but **YOU** don't get that." Rick pointed out.

"We have our moments." I replied.

"I get lists." I said.

"Lists?" Asked Rick.

"Yeah. Can I do this? Make sure you do that. Get this and get that on your way home and so on!"

"That's because you're a forgetful fucker". Rick said.

"Oh thanks."

"What's tonight all about?" Rick asked, fixing his hair in the vanity mirror.

"You know – a run through, a rehearsal, make sure everything works! That kinda shit."

"I don't rehearse. Can you do it on your own?"

"No, I can't! We need to test the sound, top brass from Top Rank will be there, and they need to be impressed."

"Top tossers." Rick snorted. Then after a significant pause, "I'll impress 'em!"

"Oh shit." I thought. Rick's idea of impressing someone isn't everyone's idea of being impressed. But I knew I could trust him. Maybe he would just show off a bit more than normal, jump a bit higher, snarl a bit more than usual.

Rick had other ideas.

We arrived to scenes of sheer panic. Nothing was ready. Cardboard boxes, opened and flattened, were everywhere, glasses were being unpacked and stacked in the bar, spirits and optics were still being installed, there was sawdust all over the floor, the smell of fresh varnish, (Rick loved that) and the paint still wet. It looked a million miles from being ready.

Gary came rushing over.

"Don't worry, we're not on till nine."

"Nine?" I said, eyes popping out.

"This won't be ready till nine next Friday."

"No, they've assured me we are good to go at nine tonight. A full show, routines from the bar staff, everything."

"Gary, we don't do cabaret." I protested.

"No, no." He spluttered. "It's just for tonight, the top knobs want to see everything. Tomorrow and Saturday, it's all yours." He assured us.

"Fucking better be." Rick said, "Or we're off aren't we bud?" He looked at me.

"It'll be okay." Gary said to Rick.

"Where's Craig?" I asked. "Do you know where we're staying?"

"Yes, the Regent. It's just around the corner; five minutes tops."

The Regent was a rundown Rank hotel, so it cost them nothing to put us in there.

That made sense.

"Hope it's got a minibar." Rick said.

"Keep it together this weekend for God's sake." Gary said, getting agitated.

"He will." I replied.

"Need us before nine?" I asked.

"Be here at eight at the latest. I want you to meet Ted and some of the top brass, tell them what this is all about. It's a completely new concept for the office bods and they'll want to say hello and see where their money is going."

"Coming from." Rick said.

"Eh?" Gary looked bemused.

"Coming from." Rick repeated. "They'll be happy on Saturday night when they're counting their dosh. Fucking greedy bastards, the lot of them."

"Alright Rick, just behave this weekend. It's very important." Gary said with a touch of fear in his voice.

"Relax Gary I'll keep my shit together; you just keep yours, and make sure we get paid."

"Enough Rick. We'll get paid. Come on let's eat." I said, heading for the door.

The Regent was very rundown, very seedy. Obviously in its heyday it took pride of place in splendid opulence. Now faded, forgotten, overtaken by new modern upstarts, shining chrome and steel but they wouldn't last the one hundred or so years the Regent had. The lifts had metal gates that creaked, and groaned, and protested, but inside the hotel was generally clean. We checked in and found our room on the first floor. Two double beds with folded towels placed neatly on each one, and a small bar of soap on top of them.

"Great!" said Rick. "Two DOUBLE beds this time. Someone in Rank will get a bollocking for spending too much on this one."

"Shite!" Came too soon after "Great."

"What?" I asked.

"No minibar, just a fridge with fuck all in it."

"Knew it was too good to be true, bastards." Rick complained.

"Never mind," I said cheerfully, "at least we have a tab in the bar, and I'm starving. Come on let's check out the restaurant."

Rick cheered up immediately and headed for the door. We found Ray and Paul already digging into ribs and fries.

"Hi guys." I said, "You must've got here nice and early."

"Hi," Rick said, "and two of those for me," to anyone who might, remotely, look like they were taking an order.

"Shit, you been in there?" Paul asked.

"Yeah I know," I nodded, "but I guess it's always like this before an opening. Remember Hemel?"

"Yeah they were still stapling beavers to the walls the night before." Rick reminded us.

Various stuff, recognizable, and some unrecognizable. ('Animalarna,' as Rick called it.)

"Well we just gotta run through it tonight. If anything is going to go wrong, it'll go wrong tonight, so no stress." I reassured them.

"Two dry whole racks and two fries," Rick ordered "and what you having?" He asked me.

I thought he'd ordered for both of us, but obviously he was just having them both for himself.

"Just one of the same for me." I said.

"And four beers please". Rick ordered. "That's one each." Rick protested after he noticed me glaring at him. There'll be plenty on tap the whole weekend I assured him.

"Effing better be." Rick said holding off the F word for the waitress's sake.

"That'll be all?" She asked.

Ray and Paul grunted and nodded in perfect unison, a typical bass and drum trait, even kept time whilst eating. If I counted, I bet they would be at exactly the same place through their racks.

Wonderful.

"Well this is great." I said.

Rick looked around as if the food had suddenly arrived.

"This is great isn't it?" I repeated. "Loads of work, stuff we like playing and a great future ahead."

I felt like their dad. Congratulating them on some great achievement, patting them on their backs.

"Great." said Ray. God, him and Paul would win gold on synchronized anything. They both finished their ribs at exactly the same time. Our food arrived and you'd think Rick hadn't eaten for a week. He finished his two racks in the same time I ate my one. At least it might soak up some beer later.

It didn't.

Chapter 6

We went back to our rooms to catch a quick nap. Rick using headphones, was still too loud to sleep.

"Rick! Come on man!"

"EH?" He shouted loudly, as he couldn't hear himself.

I pointed to both my ears, hoping he'd understand but he just took them off and offered them to me.

"Great, aren't they?" He shouted again, "Aerosmith. Love 'em!" He was still shouting.

"No." I said. "Turn them down. I'm trying to kip!"

"Oh ok." He sounded disappointed at my lack of interest. I love Aerosmith too, but time and place etc....

We wandered over to the venue just before eight, after meeting Ray and Paul in the hotel bar. Still carnage in there more 'stuff' appeared to be nailed to the walls, electricians on those platforms on wheels that extend right up to the high ceilings, were positioning spots to shine on the stage area. The bar was piled high with every kind of boxed glass. The silhouette printed on the outside give a clue to what was on the inside. There must have been hundreds of them, boxes I mean, with six, eight, or twelve glasses neatly packed inside.

Mirrors were being cleaned; copper artefacts were being polished. It still didn't look anywhere near finished to me, but these things have a knack of pulling themselves together at the last minute and I was sure it would be fine. Gary had spotted us, he was with Craig from Rank and another 'Top Tosser' as Rick called them and was making his way over to us.

"Hi lads." Gary said. "This is Craig who you've met, and this is Ted, head of entertainment for Rank."

"Yo!" we all said. and shook hands, Gary introducing us as we did so. Ted gave us an up and down, suspicious look.

"Don't worry we'll have our stage togs on for tomorrow and Saturday." I reassured him.

"Oh…Oh that's good." Ted relaxed a little.

"So, what's happening tonight then?" I asked.
Craig took over and told us certain guests would be allowed in at nine, and then the night was to run as a normal night. They had been given £20 to spend at the bar. Any hiccups could be sorted out as we go, so on the real opening night, all should be running smoothly. We were given the running order which would be controlled by the DJ acting as MD and compere for the night. DJ 'Smokescreen' was one of the best. We'd worked with him often and suggested him for this job. He was really grateful and continually sent drinks over to us from that night onwards.

"What the fuck is the 'Hillbillies on fire routine'?" Rick asked, looking at the running order for this evening.

"Rick!" I said, putting my fingers to my lips as I tried to reign him in a tad.

"Oh you'll love it!" Enthused Ted.

"Will I?" Rick said as deadpan as Rick could be.

"Yeah it's real rooting tooting stuff, one I thought of myself." Said Ted with a real beam all over his face.

"Oh Shi__"

"RICK!" I stopped him., "I'm sure it'll go down a storm." I reassured Ted.

"ONE TWO, ONE TWO" blasted out from the P. A. Once again Crown amps married to JBL speakers. Nearly everyone jumped, as it raced over our heads, hit the back wall and raced back a nanosecond later, creating a great delay effect.

"That might be a problem". Said Ray.

"No, the monitors will solve that". I said.

"Just make sure you get your own custom sound on stage and it'll be fine."

"If you say so." Said Ray, not quite convinced.

"Ok everyone," asked Smokescreen, "can we have you all gathered around the front of house, and I'll let you know what's occurring." He ran through the night's order of play, told everyone to clean up the mess and leave what they were doing, get changed, and report back to the DJ console.

"Can we do a quick sound check?" I asked him.

"Yeah. Sure man! How are you guys doing? Thanks for the gig mate, it's going to be awesome."

Ray bashed each drum separately, shouting orders at Smokescreen, who was frantically twiddling knobs and instructing his little helper, who was positioning mics, and running back and forward.

Ray had a larger than normal bass drum, for depth, but liked a lot of top (treble) on the EQ, it wasn't known as a kick drum for nothing. Ray's bass drum really kicked. Paul played some bass, and then Ray and Paul played together. I could hear Smokescreen making adjustments until it suddenly gelled together. Nods from Ray and Paul confirmed everything sounded good.

Rick slammed his left hand down onto the keyboard as hard as he could. G, two octaves below middle C, and the G, an octave lower. This was his default sound checker. He knew instantly what was needed as he heard this octave thunder out. Rick looked at Smokescreen, who was leaning over the mixing desk, both hands frantically twiddling knobs, then he pushed the slider up, and signalled to Rick to do it again.

Rick did it again, this time it really rocked. Just the two notes on the Roland piano and masses of power amp back up, made Rick raise his eyebrows, and I thought I saw him smile for a moment. A wry one at that. Rick give him a nod, and I turned to my piano, played a few riffs and runs, Smokescreen twiddled, and twitched, then looked at me as if to say 'ok'?

I nodded, we did a quick 'one two' into the radio mics, and Rick took off with 'Whole Lotta Shakin', no intro just started it. Sixteen bars in, Paul, Ray, and I came in on the dot and we were off. It sounded great. I knew that because Rick started dancing as he played, an infectious movement of swaying, foot tapping, lifting one leg sometimes, arching over the piano, like some demented horror movie star, playing an organ. He just needed his hoodie and the part would have been complete.

Everyone stopped what they were doing and watched. All of them copying Rick's movements, some people started jiving and swinging together. Rick started singing and it was complete. Four guys playing as tight as it gets, with enough energy to power the whole site. I spotted Gary, Craig, and Ted in a line by the far wall. Gary and Craig swaying, and foot tapping in perfect time. Ted standing stone still like a statue but with his mouth wide open. I took that as a good sign, and I thought "Poor Ted should get out more."

We finished 'Whole Lotta Shakin' with Rick's leap into the air. He came down bang on time, to an arousing crescendo 'splat' of a chord, and Ray and Paul stopping too, at a predetermined moment we just felt was right. Luckily, we always got it right. Tight as a dovetail, then a nanosecond of silence before the crowd, the staff, I should say, burst out into enthusiastic applause, whooping and shouting, then gathering themselves soberly, remembering that their bosses were there.

Gary gave me a "yes" sign with his fist, arm bent up in front of him and a big smile on his face. Craig slapped him on the back and Ted shouted "YO!" and almost frightened himself.

"Great!" Said Smokescreen over the mics. "The Duelling Pianos everyone," and the clapping started again. "Can we have the Hillbillies up next please?"

"I'm off to the bog." Rick announced.
Gary plus two came over to the stage. Gary was beaming. Craig seemed satisfied, and even Ted held out his hand and said, "Wow! That was something." Then my heart sank.

"Fucking Hillbillies on Fire my arse." Came over the speakers. Then a door slamming. Everyone stopped to see where it was coming from. Then the most enormous breaking of wind, followed by what can only be described as the dump of all dumps.

Rick was in the toilet.

He didn't know he'd left his mic on, and it was still being picked up by the wireless pickups. Smokescreen wasn't at his station, so Rick was not faded out. I then spotted him at the side of the stage, out of sight to everyone off the stage, splitting his sides laughing and gesturing to me as if to say, "Don't tell anyone you can see me!"

He didn't want to turn Rick down.

"Cocksuckers the lot of them". Came over the speakers with more strains and dumps.

"Fuck!" Then "Urrrggghhh," then more dumps. Smokescreen was beside himself, on his knees, convulsed in uncontrollable laughter. I went over to the mixing desk ignoring Smokescreen's "NO! NO! let it run!" Tears were streaming down his cheeks. I pulled the master fader down and Rick went silent.

Gary and Craig got it, and tried to control themselves. Ted thought it was part of 'Hillbillies on Fire', and shrugged his shoulders. A loud chatter went up in the room with lots of giggles, and shrieks of laughter. The Hillbillies did their stuff. Smokescreen trying to mix it but still in tears.

Rick came back in.

"Washed your hands?" Shouted Smokescreen over the PA, just about managing to control himself.

The staff stood applauding to a bemused Rick who said to me, "What the fuck's going on?"

"Your mic was live when you were in the loo!" I explained. "We got the whole performance."

"Shit!" Said Rick.

"Yes, you certainly did." I said.

"Well if one good thing has come out of tonight that was it." Said Craig. "Just make sure you turn off your mics when you've finished." He said. "I'll tell the DJ to check also."

"He might not." I said.

"Eh?" Craig asked.

"Oh, nothing." I said, trying to stifle a laugh.

"What? You heard the whole thing?" Asked Rick as we headed for the dressing room.

"Yep!" I said, "twenty thousand watts of Rick having a dump. It was quite something! With added delay too. It was bonkers!"

"Oh fuck." Said Rick not really giving one.

"I'll remember next time."

"Smokescreen refused to turn you off. I thought he was going to have a thrombie."

"What? He knew?"

"Yep. I've never seen anyone laugh that much in all my life."

"Little fucker." Rick said, "Wait till I see him."

"Oh come on let's grab a drink, we'll have to do the whole caboosh again soon. Nice soundcheck by the way"

"Yeah! It was sick wasn't it?"

"It was huge." I said, patting him on the back.

"I'm just going to ring Yvonne and say good night to Ed. He'll love what I'm about to tell him. See you at the bar."

"Yes, Ed WILL love that." Rick said "Faeces and all, ha ha." He added sarcastically.

"Hi babe!" Yvonne answered. "How's it going?"

"How did you know it was me?"

"Always know it's you when you ring." She said

"Yeah, it's going great, a few hic ups but all should be okay tonight. You'll never guess what happened with Rick?"

"Oh no, is he locked up?"

"No. But he was locked in when this happened, and I ran through the whole episode, Yvonne was in hysterics.

"Flaming typical! Only Rick could do that!"

Ed came on and I went through the whole story with him, changing the word to poo as required. I thought Ed was going to wet himself.

"Dad!" He said "NO! Poor Rick, and everyone heard him?"

"Yep at volume number 11!" I said.

"Awwwww, poor Ricky. But I bet he didn't give a poo did he dad?"

"Ha ha!" I laughed at Ed, changing the word for me.

"Off to bed." I said. Love you, and see you Sunday afternoon for birthday brunch."

"Yay! OK." He sounded excited.

"Look after Mum." I said.

"I will. I'm the man of the house when you're not here Dad, remember?"

"Sure, big boy". I said.

I always told Ed he was the man of the house when I was out, and he took it so seriously.

"Night Dad. Here's Mum."

"Go on I'll be up in a minute and clean those teeth."

Then in unison I heard them both say,

"The bottoms of the tops and the tops of the bottoms." We used to say this to Ed, so he didn't miss any out.

"Hi, sorry babe." Yvonne said.

"Oh, I miss you two so much." I said. "Can't wait for Sunday."

"It will come sooner than you think."

Yvonne said being ever so cheerful and positive.

"I can come back after the gig Saturday, but they've got this big corporate party afterwards, and I think I should stay and show my face. You know do a bit of networking and so on."

"No that's fine Hun." Yvonne said. "You do it and enjoy it. Birthday brunch will be good."

"Ok, better go and check on Rick. It's a free bar".

"Oh my God. Good luck with that one!"

"He'll be okay. He was awesome at the rehearsal."

"Thought Rick didn't rehearse!" Yvonne exclaimed.

"Well he doesn't need to rehearse his dumps! God knows what Son feeds him!"

We laughed, and said our goodbyes and love yous, and blew kisses. We both hung up.

Rick was the leaning on the bar with three female Hillbillies, hanging on every word, enjoying his captive audience immensely, until Craig walked past, clapping his hands very loudly and shouting, "Come on work to be done!"

"See you later." They all said simultaneously, one of them touching Rick's arm and only letting go at the last minute, as she walked away backwards, hanging on until she could no longer reach him.

"It's the black leather jacket." I said.
Rick always wore black. Usually leather, sometimes silk, or suede.

"Bollocks," He retorted, "it's my raw sex appeal. Works every time."

"It's the leather!" I said stroking his arm mockingly.

"You'll probably end up with that one," I said nodding towards the last hanger on, who was now behind the bar, giving Rick the biggest 'come on' smile.

"One?" Said Rick.
Oh no, I was in for a heavy weekend. Hope they take him home so I can get some sleep. If Rick brought anyone back, I'd hide under my duvet and try not to listen. The orgasms would rise to a crescendo like Tchaikovsky's 1812. I swear I could hear cannons sometimes. God knows what he was doing with them. That was Rick's favourite, one and only, composer, he'd tell me. He often had sex to Tchaikovsky playing at volume number 11. He told me he once ran a Bistro just outside Camden Market, well he played there, on the Chalk Farm road, and persuaded the owner to let

him open it on a Saturday morning, for breakfast and brunch and he would 'do the music'. The owner agreed, and popped in to see how it was going on the first morning. He was probably expecting Rick at the piano. To his horror Rick had Tchaikovsky playing over the sound system, so loud, the customers had to shout out their orders, but there were customers! Six on the first day. After six weeks there was a queue. No one complained. No one asked for the music to be turned down. No one asked for a different composer. No one didn't finish their breakfast. Many I suspected didn't know it was all one man's work, just enjoyed yet another quirky Camden Market vibe. Rick was in his element, until the owner got bored with his Bistro, financed by his rich parents, and decided to turn it into a cocktail bar, ripping out the interior and getting some poncy designer, straight out of college, to design a 'sophisticated' cocktail bar.

"Man, he ruined it." Rick would reminisce.

"Pinpoint lights in the ceiling, purple walls, red furniture, it looked like a fucking brothel!"

I thought Rick would have liked that.

"Totally fucking ruined it, the sick bastard, and I was doing so well with "Pete" (Rick was apparently on first name terms with Pyotr Ilyich Tchaikovsky)

"Please can we have a quiet weekend?" I asked.

"Oh yeah it's your birthday isn't it? Man, you're really getting old if you want a quiet weekend."

We did the rehearsal night. It went well, everyone was pleased. Ted said thanks to everybody and, "break a leg tomorrow."

"I'll break his fucking leg." Rick mumbled, having the utmost distaste for anything corporate.
Except the bar tab.

"Come on." I said. "Let's see what's still open. It wasn't that late, and we were still wired from the playing. Rick looked towards the bar for his sex for the night, but all the staff were grouped in the centre of the dancefloor with Craig in the middle, obviously debriefing everyone and explaining what he wanted tomorrow.

"Come on Rick." I said. "We have all weekend."

Ray and Paul went for an early night, saying they wanted to go out sightseeing in the morning. They got on really well and would pair off and do their own thing in between playing. Rick and I found a quiet late-night bar still open, and grabbed a few shots, before hitting the hay. Rick tried to get the hotel bar open for a nightcap, but the night porter was having none of it. Thank God I thought, Rick had consumed copious amounts of alcohol this evening, and you wouldn't think he'd touched a drop.

Chapter 7

"Off you go, see you later." Yvonne shouted.
Ed stopped and said, "Oh mum, I'm sad of dad missing his birthday breakfast, he loves it."

"I know honey, maybe we'll make it a special brunch instead. We can still have pancakes, and bacon, and maple syrup!"

"Ok." Ed said, and turned towards the school gate "Bye mum. Love you."

"Bye darling, love you too, see you at three."
Yvonne watched Ed run off with his left arm held up high, the middle two fingers tucked in, and the end two out straight. I wasn't sure Ed knew what it meant, but he was just happy he could do something that Rick did. Yvonne went off to visit her mum.
Rick was still out for the count as I put the hotel TV on to catch up on some news.

"Aw man." He protested.

"You were asleep." I said.

"No, I wasn't," blurring his speech a little.

"Well you're the only one I know who snores when he's awake."

"Not fucking funny." Rick said, heaving himself over and completely disappearing under the duvet.
The News was boring as usual, but the weather looked great.

"Coming out?" I asked him.

"Nah." came a muffled mumble from his bed.

"Breakfast finishes soon."

"Oh shit." Came another muffle, and Rick was out of bed.

"Not missing a free breakfast." He said, heading for the bathroom.

"Especially from Rank."

We met Ray and Paul finishing off their full Englishes.

"Sleep well?" Asked Ray.

"Yeah not bad thanks. You?"

"Yeah was ok, nice and quiet. Last night was great, by the way." I said to them both.

"Aw thanks." As they both put their thumbs up.
In unison of course.

"What you two up to today?" I asked Paul.

"Probably look around the lanes do a bit of shopping, looks good for a walk along the pier". He looked at Ray and they both nodded.
In time.
Rick let out a long noisy yawn.

"What you doing then?" Ray asked.

"Back to bed I think." Rick answered. Looking around for someone he could order double everything from.

We finished our breakfasts.

Rick went back to bed. I went out for a walk.

It was a crisp autumn day and the sea was well up. I went to the end of the pier and rang Yvonne.

"Hi babe". She answered.

"You really do know when it's me don't you?"

"Of course!"

"What if you say, "Hi babe," to the headmaster?"

"No, I know when it's him". She said.

"What? The headmaster rings you?"

"No! Silly I'm just teasing you; he never rings. Why should he?"

"Had me worried for a moment then". I said.

"Silly you. How's it going?"

"The run through was fine, everyone loved it. I'm looking forward to tonight, it's on Southern, but I don't think you can get it, I'll get someone to record it for you."

"Oh great! Ed will love that."

"How is the chunky monkey?" I asked.

"He's fine. Missing you, but not as much as I am, and he's a bit upset you'll miss your birthday breakfast."

"Well, tell him it's okay we'll have a nice afternoon brunch or cream tea."

"Not the same, you know Ed. Daddy this, Daddy that!"

"He he, that's my boy! And you're okay?"

"Yeah just off to Mum's. Ricky behaving?"

"Yes, not too bad really. He's gone back to bed after getting his money's worth out of Rank at breakfast. Scoffed the lot twice!"

"Typical. I don't know where he puts it, the skinny little thing! Sonja rang for a chat last night. She really misses him, but I think she's okay. I'll tell her you said he was behaving."

"Ok. Say Hi to your mum, and drive carefully."

"I will sweetheart, have a good day and let me know how it goes. Speak tomorrow. Love you!"

"Love you!" I said and I heard the click as Yvonne hung up. I always waited for that click.

I walked around for a couple of hours. I really fancied a coffee but was still too full, from breakfast, so I went for a laydown. Rick was out, so I laid on my newly made bed and went off to sleep. Rick woke me up coming in noisily, and with a loud rustling of shopping bags.

"Hiya mate." He said, not seeming to notice I may have been sleeping.

"Where have you been?" I asked him. Not moving.

"Out shopping, there is a great joke shop in the Lanes. They've got everything."

"Everything?" I asked nervously.

"Yeah. Costumes and stuff. I bought something for tonight, should be fun."

"What is it?" I asked.

"Oh, you'll see, later." He said, with the wickedest of grins.

Oh no, I thought, what's he up to now?
This can only be trouble.
I had no idea how much trouble it was going to be.
No idea.

"Fancy a wander over to the venue to see how it's going?" Rick asked.
Not like him to be keen on anything practical.

"Oh, are those chicks working?" I asked.
Rick looked hurt.

"I don't know." He said. "Just thought we could go and check it out."
He was probably just bored and wanted something to do. Somewhere to go.

"Ok." I said, jumping off the bed.
There was something large in the shopping bag, which was covered in every different clown's face imaginable. Oh, dear I thought. What is he up to?

"What's in there?" I asked, pointing at the bag.

"Not much." He said, kicking it under the bed.

"Come on, I fancy going out."
We checked in at the venue. Same mayhem, clutter everywhere, people frantically running around in a blind panic. The smell of fresh paint and varnish and bleach.

"Hi!" Called out Gary.

"Hiya buddy"." I said, "All going okay?"

"Yep, all good." He said.

"Can you guys be here, by six sharp? Southern are doing a live broadcast from here, and they want you two playing out the show. We shall be on the local 6.30 bulletin. This'll be great publicity for the venue."

"Sure". I said, "I'll make sure we're all here at six."

"Fully dressed and everything." Gary ordered.

"Of course." I said. "I get it."

"Good man." he said "Must get on - Ted's freaking out a bit. I've told him everything is on track, if not we shall stuff all the mess in a cupboard, out of sight and sort it tomorrow!"

"Sounds about right! I said. "Oh No!"

"What's up?" Asked Gary.

"Look at Rick." I said.

He was behind the bar, standing behind the girl that had the hots for him last night. His arms inside her jumper. They were both enjoying themselves obviously.

"Tell him that's sexual harassment," Gary said, "and get him the fuck out from behind the bar. Ted will do his nut."

"On my way."

I guess it would have been sexual harassment but with Rick, the girls didn't seem to mind.

"Rick!"

"Whassup man?" He asked, innocently.

"Get out of there!" I said, "You'll get done."

"Aw Mate," Rick protested, "see you later honey," he said to the girl who looked a bit miffed

"You bet." She said. Grabbing his balls and squeezing them. Rick looked like he was having an orgasm.

"Out! Now!" I said.

"Okay, okay," I'm coming."

"I know." Said the girl, letting him go with a pat on his backside.

"See YOU later". She said, with a drop-dead gorgeous smile. Rick was now on the correct side of the bar, a little flustered, but beaming with confidence.

"Oh, there goes my sleep." I said, "Maybe I should get another room?"

"No," Rick said, "You can watch!" He said, meaning it.

"Watch and learn." He said, trying to keep a straight face.

"Do me a favour", I said.

"What?" Asked Rick.

"Aw, just do me a favour, have a night off."

"Night off? What's up with you?"

"Come on, a quick nap. I'll tell the others that we have to be here at six sharp, for Southern."

"Southern?" Rick asked.

"Oh sorry. Forgot to tell you. We are on the 6.30 News. Just have to run through the song as the program ends. Probably while the credits are running. They're doing a big item on the whole venue opening, how good it is for the town and so on."

"We're going to be on the telly?"

"Yeah, and it's Live, so fucking behave. I'm serious."

"Ok cool man. I'll behave".

"Thanks," I said. "we don't want to blow this one, just do your usual stuff, and be professional."

"Which song do you think we should do?" I asked.

"Great Balls, don't you think? It's instantly recognizable, no intro, just straight in."

"You're right." I said, marvelling how Rick could be a real pro, most of the time.

"And get all the staff available around the piano for effect". He added.

"Wow! You're really on it today."

"Well maybe Ed'll see it, and I want him to be proud of his uncle Rick."

Eh? Not Sonja? I thought, and I didn't mind him referring to himself as Uncle Rick. Ed knew he wasn't his real uncle, but they both had that kind of relationship, and I didn't think twice about it.

"That's nice of you." I said. "Thanks. I'll try and get someone to record it as it's not on up there."

"Brill. You hungry?"

Hungry? I thought. How could he be hungry after what he put away earlier?

"Actually, yeah. Burger?"

"Now you're talking." He said. "Let's try one of the new places on site."

"Yeah. Sounds good. Let's go." I said.

Some food outlets were open. Doing the same as we did yesterday, serving anyone who was around, just to check systems, ovens, fryers, and so on.

"That was fab". Said Rick, followed by the most gut-wrenching burp I'd ever heard.

"Rick!" I said. "Keep it in."

"Better out than in." He said.

Was it? I thought. We wandered back to the Hotel. Ray and Paul were sitting in the lobby having coffee. They looked like two guys on holiday together, enjoying some down time.

"Hi, how's it going?"

"Yeah, great." They said simultaneously nodding in exact time together.

"Where did we find you two?" I asked.

"Eh?" They both said in time again.

"Never mind. We have to be over there fully dressed at six, for a live TV. Southern are doing an item on the news, and we have to play a song to show them what we do."

"Ok." Came back from the duo.

"See you here at quarter to?"

"Yep sure." They said.

"I'm off for a quick kip."

"See you later mate". Came back in perfect unison. Rick was trying to get a drink at the bar.

"Oi! Come on". I said. Pointing upstairs.

"Aw man." Rick protested.

Six o'clock sharp we walked into the venue and the Duelling Pianos bar.

"Wow!" Rick said, "What happened to all that shit?"

The place looked spotless; everything was gleaming like new. Some last-minute polishing going on and "DANGER! WET FLOORS" signs everywhere.

"Hi Sweetie." Came from the bar.

"Hi!" Said Rick, and was just about to make his way over to her.

"Rick!" I said, "This way."

Rick blew her a kiss and raised his eyes to heaven. As if to say, sorry I have to go.

"See you later." He said.

"Oh yes you will." Rick looked chuffed.

"Come on." I said let's get ready."

In the dressing room a TV guy came in with headphones on, and a clipboard, looking really tense and stressed beyond belief. Bet he smokes 40 a day I thought.

"Right guys. Hi, I'm Andy, floor manager for tonight. What we want is on my count for you to kick off and do one minute 45 seconds exactly. You must start exactly on my count as it will be a direct handover from the studio, and we mustn't have the slightest gap. Understand? I will count you in with a 5.4.3.2.1." He demonstrated with his fingers his silent count down and then said,

"Then you start exactly as I finish. Not a nanosecond before or after. Got it?"

"Yeah." Said Rick, surprising everyone. "I'll start on the dot and do my jump at 1 minute 43 seconds. I'll count it in my head. We should stop bang on time at one minute 45 seconds. Should be time for a verse and a quick one - two on the pianos. Just keep watching me, it'll be okay".

"Sure?" Asked Andy.

"Yep, sure." Said Rick.

Wow, I thought, Rick was really stepping up to the mark.

"Ok, meet you by the piano at 6.20 latest. We'll have a monitor on stage you can see the whole item. I can get it close to you er……"

"Rick." Said Rick.

"I can get it close to you Rick, and you can watch the clock on screen. You'll be able to see 6. 30. 00 exactly and that's when you stop."

"Ok, thanks." Said Rick. "But you probably won't need it." He added.

"I'll make sure it's there anyway. Everyone good? Any questions?"

We all looked at each other shaking our heads.

"Okay. Great. See you out there". Said Andy, nodding towards the stage.

"Oh, and by the way," he said, halfway out of the door,

"Yeah?" Asked Rick.

"Break a leg!" He said before leaving in a hurry, getting trapped in the closing door, and angrily shoving himself out through it.

"Poor sod," Rick said. "See what corporate shit does to you? I bet he was a cool guy."

"He is." I said. "He was alright. Explained it all to us very well. We didn't know about count ins and split-second timings." I said, "he was really helpful."

"Yeah, I suppose so." Rick said. "Just feel sorry for him."

This was not like Rick. Oh well maybe he was maturing, growing up, calming down a bit.

Rick wasn't.

Six twenty. We were on set. Ray and Paul were ready for our cue. We could see on the monitor, placed at the end of Rick's piano, two talking heads introducing film clips of the venue's other facilities. Bar managers doing their 'Live' feed. Ted beaming, as he was being interviewed, looking so proud of himself. He'd actually done nothing to get this place up and running, just signed a few very large checks and drank expensive wine and ate expensive dinners, as various companies tended for their contracts, and wooed him with every extravagance going.

"Toss head." Rick said.

"Shush!" I hissed, "we might be heard!"

In the top right-hand corner, there was a digital clock ticking away at hyper speed 6h.25m.36sec and another, incoherent number whizzing along. These were, I guessed, tenths or even hundreds of a second blurred to the eye. At 6h.26min10sec and a blur, Andy burst into the room racing towards the stage. He'd obviously counted in everyone else and now it was close to our time.

"Yeah Roger that!" He said to no - one. Then his walkie-talkie crackled "Ready in two."

"Roger." Andy said. "Ready?"

"Yep." We said.

"At 6.28.15 exactly you start."

I'll count you in physically, at 6. 28. 10. Dead. Got it?"

"Yep, ready." Said Rick.

Ray puffed, and pulled his snare drum closer.

Paul tensed and relaxed his shoulders, letting his bass rest on his custom-made red leather strap.

"Ready in one." Crackled the walkie-talkie.

The two talking heads were having an exciting time on this news item. We couldn't hear them, but their body language said a lot. Suddenly they both looked to the monitor in the studio as the walkie-talkie crackled, "GO!"

5.4.3.2.1. Gestured Andy, who omitted the one, and got out of the way. At '2', Rick jumped into the air, came down on zero and started "Great Balls of Fire".

It thundered out. Rick's vocals on top of it. Andy's jaw dropped. Not sure if it was too loud for him, or the fact it all went right on time, or what.

Surely, he was used to this? The monitor instantly changed to a close-up of Rick's manic body over the keyboard. I hadn't noticed the handheld camera man right next to him. He panned out and caught us all coming in on time, as the song took off. He knew his stuff. The monitor showed the credits starting to roll. Shame we were on at the end. People at home might be wandering off to put the kettle on. We did a quick solo each. The cameraman instinctively knew who to follow. At 6.29. 55. Andy did his five finger count down. Rick leapt into the air and we came down right on the 0 of Andy's count. The big 'splat' chord ending, hanging as the monitor went to a commercial break.

"AND WE'RE OUT!" Crackled the walkie-talkie. "Great guys. Well done. Perfect." Andy was happy.

"Thanks! Roger that," he said, and breathed a big sigh of relief. "Brilliant! We bagged it. Well done. Thanks very much."

"A pleasure man". Rick said, slapping Andy on his back. I think Rick genuinely liked him.

"Going to be here tonight?" Asked Rick.

"Can't". Said Andy, "gotta get back and do an edit for the 10.30 Slot."

"We're gonna be on again?" Rick asked.

"Yep. Just a re - cap, but I'll make sure that your 1min,45 is in there in full. It was awesome."

"Thanks man." Rick said.

Andy scurried off to "A BEER?" From the walkie-talkie. "Yep. You can Roger that," Said Andy, getting it wrong. We hung around until the official opening at 7pm. We would be on stage at 9pm, and again at 11pm, Smokescreen would do his stuff and the Hillbillies 'on fire', would do theirs.

Rick headed for the bar, not just for a drink. He'd been great this weekend, I couldn't be angry with him. He was holding it together, playing great, working hard, and was enjoying himself. In his black leather gear, spiky hair and black Converse trainers, he looked the part. Super confident, fit, despite his lifestyle, good looking, but underneath he was vulnerable and sensitive. You would never have thought that, looking at him, but I knew him better, and we were really best mates. The Rick in the sleazy jazz club, dive bar, or wherever someone would let him play, was a world away from the Rick playing with us as a duelling pianist. Something he always thanked me for. He didn't know he had it in him. He admitted only coming to the audition for a laugh. He was bored he said, but when we played together something magical happened. I certainly felt it and thank God he did. He could have walked away, but he didn't, and he we are, having a blast.

"So, what you doing later?" Rick asked Siobhan. I now knew her name.

"Not sure." She said, making a Margarita. "Maybe if you're lucky you can get my tits out."

"Maybe if YOU'RE lucky, I will." Came back from Rick, without any hesitation.

"Your Margarita sweetie." Said Siobhan, sliding the glass towards him.

"What's this?" I asked Rick, nodding at the drink.

"Hi." I said to Siobhan.

"Same for you?" She asked me.

"Yeah why not? Thanks."

"We have to practice these so let me know what you think."

"We will." Said Rick. "Better have another one to make sure."

"Watch it." Siobhan said.

"Brown stuff." Rick replied.

"Eh?" Siobhan looked puzzled.

Rick looked at me and waved his arm straight over and just above his head.

"Missed it. Didn't she?" He said.

"Guess so."

"Here you go honey." Siobhan slipped the glass towards me.

"Cheers." I said. "Wow! Nice."

Siobhan looked pleased with herself and moved off to wash the cocktail shaker.

"Nice eh?" Asked Rick.

"Yep really tasty."

"Not the drink. Her!"

"Oh yeah! Be careful mate she's got it in for you."

"Hope so." Rick said, as he finished his drink in one swig. "Hope so."

Nine o'clock came, and Rick slammed his hand down onto his keyboard. We were off. Ray puffed, Paul bounced, and I played catch up with Rick. He was off on one tonight. Maybe the thought of Siobhan afterwards had inspired him a little. Not that he needed any inspiration. The crowd loved it. It was new to them, and they dug it straight away, all 800 of them. Gary and Craig were at the bar with the occasional thumbs up. Ted was nowhere to be seen. Rick was amazing. Eleven o'clock came, and we did it all again, different songs obviously, well some got repeated, we reckon there would be a different audience in later, and the early doors folk might not notice a repeat. We finished at midnight to that big 'splat' chord of a finish, and the crowd went bananas. We delivered the lot. At one point I felt we were Rick's backing band. He was great and he knew it. Ray and Paul went off to bed, I assumed.

I said to Rick,

"You coming? I'm knackered."

"Nah, catch you later." Said Rick, fixing his hair and making sure his jacket was hanging just right.

"Good luck." I said. "Please keep it down when you come in."

"Well, if I come in." He said, with a twinkle in his eye. I'd seen that twinkle before. Last time he disappeared for a couple of days, only to reappear, covered in bruises, well love bites really. I just shook my head.

"See you tomorrow then. Well done for tonight you were great."

"I know." Said Rick, tongue in cheek. "You weren't so bad tonight, either."

"And the boys were good." He added.

"Yep they really rock those two." I said. "Lucky for us!"

"Sure is." Said Rick. "I'm off, catch you later buddy."

"Good luck." I said, and Rick was gone. Into the night of whatever Rick's nights are like. Certainly not dull. For a moment I missed him. I felt bereft. Silly me, I thought. Smokescreen had them leaping. The last hour was always easy. The alcohol had kicked in and he knew his job. I waved goodbye as I left the stage and "See you buddy," came over the speakers, crystal clear. I gave him the two-finger salute (not the 'V' sign) and I heard him laugh over the mic. Soon I was in the land of nod, and morning came, no sign of Rick, I got a full night's sleep. Great I thought.

Now, where's breakfast.

Chapter 8

Yvonne and Ed were having breakfast together.

"Hey tiger, I've got a really good idea."

"What's that Mum?" Ed asked, already excited by a really good idea.

"Why don't we get up early tomorrow, drive down and see Daddy, take him his breakfast. We can make a flask of coffee, croissants, and pancakes and syrup, and maybe some other goodies. We'll go shopping later."

"Yeah, Dad will love that! Can we? Can we really?"

"Why not? It'll be a lovely surprise for him." Yvonne said adding, "Oh, we'll have to feed Rick too."

"Why's that?" Ed asked.

"They share a room to save money." Yvonne explained.

"What? Dad sleeps with Rick?"

"Not exactly they have their own beds." She said giggling a bit.

"Well that's alright then." Ed said, looking a bit puzzled, chomping on his Shreddies.

"Can we take Uncle Ricky some cheese puffs? You know he loves them, and maybe Sonja might want to come too."

Yvonne gave Ed a loving look. She liked his sensitivity, always thinking of others. Just like his dad she thought.

"Nah, just the two of us, on a road trip eh?"

"Yay! Great!" Ed said, "When are we going shopping?"

"Finish off," Yvonne said, "and we'll get cleaned up and go out."

"Ok, fab." Ed said, rushing to finish his Shreddies.

"Slowdown! You know what your Dad says,"

"Chew everything 42 times!" They both said in unison.

The phone rang.

"That'll be Daddy." Yvonne said looking at her watch.

"I'll get it." Shouted Ed, and ran to the phone.

"NOT A WORD!" Yvonne said.

"I know! Hi Dad, how's it going?"

"Wow! Now even you know it's me before you answer? How did you manage that?" I asked.

"Mum said it was you!" Ed replied.

"Then Mum really is psychic."

"What's that Dad? Hey Mum, dad says you're psychic what's that?" Ed asked his mum, not waiting for his dad to answer.

"Tell you later honey." Yvonne said, "Chat to Daddy, then hand him over."

"Okay. Hi Dad. Did Ricky do more farting?"

"No. He behaved." We were on the TV here last night; I'll try and get a copy for you so we can watch it when I'm back."

"Great. You'll be famous soon."

"Not sure about that. What are you up to today?"

"We are going shopping." Ed said excitedly. Then remembering he was sworn to silence, quickly added, "might get you a card if you're lucky."

"Thanks buddy, "no football this morning?"

Ed kicked around on Saturdays, but didn't really like it. Preferred being home doing 'stuff' with us, which was lovely.

"No, the pitch is water bogged" he said.

"Logged." I said trying not to let him hear me laugh.

"Logged?" Asked Ed. "No, it's water bogged! No wood there Dad, silly!"

"No, it's called waterlogged." I said. "Not water bogged."

"Oh, is it? Okay it's waterlogged," satisfied with my explanation.

Ed was always getting his words muddled.

"Where does Mummy work?" I asked.

"At the Hostable."

"Where?"

"The Hostable."

"The Hospital." I said.

"Oh yeah, there!" Said Ed. Now starting to laugh as he knew I was just teasing.

"Wanna speak with mum? She's right here."

"Okay, put her on and have a nice day. Look after Mum."

"I will dad. Love you, see you tomorrow for your birthday treat."

"Thanks buddy. Love you too."

Yvonne came on and I could hear Ed ask, "Where is it you work again mum?"

"Don't tease him like that, it's cruel." Yvonne said to me. "How are you? Was last night ok? Did Rick behave?"

"How was the hostable?" I asked.

"Stop!" Yvonne said. "You'll give him a complex."

"Did he eat his 'oghurt?" I said, starting to laugh out loud.

"Stop!" Yvonne said again. "He's only little."

"I know, just love it when he gets his words mixed up that's all. Yes, it went really well. Rick was fab as usual. Think he's pulled half of the bar crew, the female half that is. They're all over him and he didn't come back last night."

"Well you got some quality sleep then!" and after a short pause, "I hope".

"Course I did. Slept like a log till eight then remembered breakfast."

"Hotel ok? Which one is it?"

"The Regent on Broad Street. A bit tatty, but clean. Obviously seen better days."

"Rick's gonna bankrupt them with what he eats for breakfast."

"Hah! I bet. What's your room number? Might wanna send you some flowers."

"Eh? Oh yeah, forgot it was my birthday. 112 on the first floor. Rick thinks we got it by mistake from Rank, as it has two massive double beds in it. He thinks if Rank knew they'd move us to a twin with no windows, and an outside toilet."

"Well that sounds ok." Yvonne said. "What are you doing today?"

"Don't know, go get a coffee, do some people watching, check out with Gary, and see if the high and mighty are happy with us. As much as Rick hates them, I'm sure he dug deeper to show them what we can do. He's got something planned for tonight and I'm a bit nervous, but I'm sure he'll be the ever pro."

"What like? What's he got planned? Something disastrous?" Yvonne asked, sounding a little bit worried.

"Well you know Rick." l said.

"Yeah, that's why I'm concerned, especially if you're a bit nervous. What's he gonna do?"

"Don't know. Just a feeling. He came back from shopping__"

"Shopping?" Yvonne interrupted, "I didn't know Ricky did shopping!" Emphasizing the word shopping.

"Hah! I know! No, he came back with something he said he got in a joke shop. He's hidden it under the bed, said it was for tonight, and I mustn't look."

"Go have a look!" Yvonne said.

"No, I gave him my word, and anyway I'm looking forward to tonight and even the after party, strangely. You don't mind me staying on, do you?"

"Of course not darling. You've been talking about this for a long time. I'm so glad you met Rick and it's all happening for you. I really am. I know how much you love playing with Rick, and I'm pleased. He's probably got some fancy-dress outfit, a gorilla maybe, knowing him. He's really trying, isn't he? He's really into it, I'm so pleased for you."

"Oh, thank you sweetheart. Yeah, you're right. Can't wait to see what he's got up his sleeve for tonight. There's been a big buzz around here, there is talk of Rank rolling them out nationwide. Apparently, they have a lot of big impressive properties, old cinemas and stuff that they want to do something with, and I think they've been impressed with us so far. Well the numbers have been great up to now, so we'll see."

"That's fabulous darling. Just what you wanted isn't it?"

"Don't want to do all the travelling and being away."

"Yeah, but you might not have to. You could just do the openings, and you and Rick could train up other pianists to do the rest. Might even be extra work for you and Rick, sounds great!"

"Yeah you're right sweetheart. It's all good really."

"Well go and relax, get your energy up for tonight, don't overcook it. I want you tomorrow night." She said.

"Can't wait." I said. "Can't wait to see you tomorrow, sweetheart."

"It will come sooner than you think." Yvonne said.

"Yep you're right!"

Not fully understanding the implications of that last remark.

"Have a good day and I hope I get a nice card!"

Yvonne made sure Ed wasn't around and then she whispered,

"Oh, Ed's already made you a fab card. Did it at school. Even Miss Barnes came out with him yesterday and said. 'This boy's got real talent.' I was dead chuffed for him."

"Miss Barnes? Positive about something? Hah! Bet he was beaming."

"He couldn't contain himself." Yvonne said, 'Wait till Dad sees this!' He shouted to me."

"Oh, so sweet of him. Okay darling, I'm off, might call you later, if not see you tomorrow. Can't wait!"

"OK. Love you lots!"

"Love you sweetheart, bye."

I waited for Yvonne to hang up. I always wanted to hang on to the last second. Then she was gone. I headed for the nearest real coffee bar, I didn't like the big corporates, always preferred the independents. Much more personal, and the coffee was always made with love, or passion, or whatever it was. It always tasted much better than the big boys. I sipped my Mountain blend and thought how lucky I was. Doing a job I loved. Living with a woman I loved, with a son I loved, working with a guy I loved. Life felt pretty good. I watched people walking by outside, some huddled up against the cold and damp.

'A consultant'. I thought, as a guy walked past dressed in expensive Burberry. 'A lawyer', looking at a woman, with a very sharp, precise haircut, and a very expensive looking suit, and long overcoat. Probably all stressed, working more than playing, missing valuable time with their loved ones, and here's me, little old me, having a ball and getting paid for it, and time to be with my family, what could be better? I finished my second coffee. One was never enough. Why can't they make flat whites in half pint glasses?

Walking back to the venue I thought I'd buy Yvonne and Ed something from Brighton. Ed would probably like a stick of rock. He loved the fact they can get the name all the way through the middle, they were not good for his teeth though, so maybe a chocolate fire engine would do. Yvonne loved everything I bought her, just because it showed I was thinking about her. So, an oil burner, one of those little ornaments you could put some oils in the top, and a T-light underneath, would be good. We always had one going on an evening. I loved the citrusy ones. Yvonne loved

Bergamot or seaweed or fresh linen. I headed for the Lanes and found something nice for both of them. No chocolate fire engine, but a giant Kindda egg. Ed loved the little models inside. He kept them on a shelf in his bedroom, like a prized collection.

"Rick! How are you doing?" I asked him. Finding him sitting up in bed watching TV.

"Yo man, having a blast!"

"Good night?"

"Yeah, it was awesome. That Siobhan is really a goer…"

"Don't know how you do it." l said.

"Yes you do. Some just have 'it', and some don't. l just have 'it'."

"Whatcha got?" Rick asked, nodding at my bags.

"Oh, just something for Yvonne and Ed."

"Hmm, must get Son a stick of rock."

"Rick! Get her something nice! There's loads of shops out there."

"Yeah you're right." Said Rick. "I'll nip out later."

"I'm off over to the venue, see if Gary is there, wanna kick some stuff over with him. Catch you later? Maybe a burger downstairs before we start?"

"Yeah! Sounds like a plan." Rick said, "I'll leave a message for the boys."

"That's a good idea, see you around six then."

"Ok, good luck over there."

"Thanks."

I left my shopping, not under the bed. Rick could peep if he wanted. As I walked over to the venue, I wondered what tonight had in store. Rick was keeping something very quiet. Probably some anti Rank dig at someone, although I knew he wasn't stupid enough to blow our chances of more work, what I didn't know was how much my life was about to change as a result of what was in that bag; and it wasn't a gorilla suit.

I spotted Gary having a coffee in a "Frank and Benny's" one of the many food outlets battling for custom in this new shiny 'spaceship just landed' look of Rank's new project. Lots of people were wandering around, taking in the new decor. Some had ice-skates hanging around their necks, some with rolled up towels, and lots of kids with candy floss, and multi-coloured slush puppies. Ed would have loved it here. Gary saw me and beckoned me to sit down opposite him.

"Wow! Great night!" He said, "Everyone's blown away."

I assumed he meant everyone at Rank, when he said 'everyone'.

"What? The bosses? I didn't think Ted was even there." I asked.

"Yeah, he was there earlier on. He caught your first set, think he has to be home early, he does start at eight."

"Missus got him on a short lead?"

"Something like that. You know what this industry is like."

"Sure do. Rick was out all night."

"He's ok for tonight?" Gary asked, a little worried.

"Rick's always okay for tonight." l said, "You know that."

"Want one?" Gary asked, pointing to his empty cup.

"No thanks, just had two flat whites and they've hit the spot. So, any gossip?"

"Well everyone is happy. The bar manager, the venue manager, everyone. The opening was a blast. Everyone is happy with the numbers; they've beaten all targets. They know there'll be a 'honeymoon period' but they all expect it to stay high."

"How long can you do here?" He asked me.

"I thought we were just doing this weekend."

"God! I haven't even thought about the following weeks, been too busy with this place. Jeez."

"We'd rather stay at Hemel. It's 'our' place, and nearer home. Can Ian and Reg come down here for next week? They're really good and it may be good for the audience to see different faces here every week, which reminds me, we must audition new guys, especially if Rank are expanding this idea. I know a few who could, and would love to do it."

"Ok. We'll have a meet in my office Monday, I'll get Ian and Reg down for the rest of the month, would you and Rick open the new ones? It really has worked out, and you two work so well together."

"Sure. But Gary, we can see the numbers and we deserve a bit more don't you think? We can audition new guys and they'll do it for a salary, but I'm thinking door percentage for me and Rick, or at least a good hike in salary. Ray and Paul are happy. We can keep this to ourselves."

"OK. See what I can do." Gary shuffled in his chair.

"Rank shouldn't really object. They're onto a winner, and they know it." I said.

"Oh, and a small rider for the dressing room." I added, "a couple of beers each and some Coke or Pepsi and maybe sparkling water. A fridge would be good. Just something as a perk to the job. The boys would like that."

"Ok, got it." Gary said. "You coming to the party debrief later? Should be a lot of back patting for all of you, and I know there's food and a free bar."

"You bet. Hope the bar is big enough for Rick!"

"Hah! Don't know where he puts it." Said Gary.

"That was funny with the toilet…" I reminded Gary.

"Oh my God. I nearly died. Ted thought it was part of some routine. Didn't get it at all!" Gary was in tears.

"I know! Right over his head!"

"Ok, good luck tonight, and I'll see you afterwards. Where is it? In the bar?"

"Yes, everyone is having their own after do as a thank you from Rank for all their hard work." I said. "See you then."

I went back to the hotel. Rick was out. I was tempted to look under his bed but resisted. I stretched out onto mine and fell fast asleep.

Chapter 9

"Look what I got man!" Rick announced, waltzing into the room, oblivious of anyone who might be trying to sleep.

"Rick!" I protested.

"Sorry, but it's gone five, and I thought you'd want to be up now anyway. Look at this!" And he held up the scantiest piece of underwear I'd ever seen. All black lace with a small red rose in the middle of the top hem, tiniest of bra size, and "Look! poppers!" He then popped open the bottom with a triumphant "Ta da!"

"Son will never get into that." I said.

"It's for Siobhan, Got Son this," and he pulled out of another bag a large teddy with a red heart on it.

"Oh, she'll like that." I said, sarcastically.

"And this is for Ed. A huge stick of pink rock with 'Brighton' all the way through it."

"You're not giving him that."

"Oh, go on, you straight fuck. He'll love it. Take him a week to eat it!"

"No way Man, that's just too much, it'll do his teeth in."

"Aw, I want to take him something back."

"Take one of those freebie, handout Top Rank mugs. He'll love one of those. He'll think it's cool, and even cooler coming from you."

"Top Rank mug? I'll see if I can take off the Rank, and he'll have a 'Top' mug. Much cooler." Rick said.

"Don't be silly. They are glazed over."

"Alright then, I'll eat the rock myself. Come on, the boys are already waiting for us downstairs."

"I said six to them."

"It's 5:30 now. Come on we'll have a starter."

I don't know how Rick does it. He'd eat a starter, everyone else's starter, then a main, usually a burger or a pizza, then finish everyone else's mains, especially the crusty edges that people leave.

He even stopped a waitress once, who was returning to the kitchen with empties and grabbed a half empty plate from her, and ate that!

We found Ray and Paul, in the restaurant with menus in their hands.

"Yo!" they both said, in unison.

"Hi guys how's it going"?

"Great. Looking forward to tonight." Paul said.

"Yeah, great venue." Ray added, "We doing this one regularly?"

"Dunno yet. They want us to do another weekend or two here, but I said I prefer Hemel, what do you think? And also, they want us to open all the new ones they are planning on rolling out."

"Great." came the unified reply.

"I don't mind sticking with Hemel," Ray said. "It's 'our' place really, isn't it? And I know you like getting home, Chris."

"Yeah you're right there."

"How's Ian and Reg getting on in Hemel?" Paul asked.

"They're okay. Gary said the numbers were off a bit last night. The locals knew we wouldn't be there. I've also asked for a bit more money for us. Rank are creaming it in."

"Great." came in unison.

"And a rider in the contracts for drinks in the dressing room, and a fridge maybe."

"That's a good idea." Ray said "And thanks. A bit more dosh will always help."

"Well don't hold your breath." I added.

"Double quarter pounder with triple fries, coleslaw, another coleslaw, and a Becks."

"Please". Rick added, to a waitress who had suddenly appeared at our table.

"Are you coming to see us tonight?" he asked her, putting on his charm, and his little boy look, I'd seen him use dozens of times before.

"Who is 'us'?" She asked him, but looked at me for my order.

"We're at Rank." Rick said, "We're gigging there tonight."

The waitress gave me a nod as if to ask, "What are you having?"

"Cheeseburger, fries, and a side salad please."
"Drink?"
"Er, Diet Coke, please."
"Same for us two." Ray added.
They even ordered for each other now.

"You the Hillbillies on Fire?" She asked all of us, not paying too much attention to Rick.

"Fuck off!" Rick said.

"Rick!" I said to Rick.

"Sorry." I said to the waitress.

"Yeah sorry." Said Rick, puzzled at the lack of interest coming from her… "But have you seen them? They're__"

"I'll be right back with your order." And she turned and scooted off.

"Ha ha!" said Ray. "Where's your allure now then? Big boy."

"Ha ha hilarious….! Your face!"

"Probably a lezzie." Rick said. Which was his explanation of anyone who didn't fancy him or noticed him.

"Probably got some sense, more like." Ray added.

She came back with the food, completely ignoring Rick. I could see he didn't like this. I gently tapped his leg with my foot under the table, and gave him my 'behave, will you' look.

Rick rolled his eyes and started on his fries before she had even put them on the table.

"Enjoy." She said, and she was gone.

"No, I wouldn't like anything else." Rick mumbled. "Any sauces maybe? Salt? Butter? Ketchup?" Rick was mimicking, as he stuffed fries into his mouth.

"What?"

"It's all there." I said, pointing to a small carousel of condiments at the end of the table. Rick shrugged his shoulders and finished the first portion of fries.

We ate our food. Rick surveying the other plates for any scraps. There weren't any.

"Come on," I said, "Let's go and do this."

Chapter 10

"Wow!" Said Ray, "Look at that."
There was a queue of at least 100 yards or more at the main entrance, with security guys saying, "Jumping Jacks only; cinema goers and everyone else go straight in."
Inside, the queue veered off to the left, and stopped at the entrance to our venue.
It was only 7.30.

"Why don't they just let them in?" Rick asked, "Start selling some juice."
I knew he didn't mean orange.

"Probably not ready I guess." I replied.
We walked right to the front and were allowed in much to the annoyance of the people at the front, judging by the looks we got.

"It's the band." Said a voice from behind the security glass. "We'll be opening soon. The floor is still a bit wet, should be fine in a minute."

Everything looked great. Clean, and still looking brand-new. Smokescreen had some moody lighting on, and cool sounds at a low level coming from the speakers. Those JBL's were so good at any volume, more like a very expensive home stereo than a concert

PA system. I gave him the thumbs up as I crossed the stage, en route to our dressing room. He gave me the 'cool' two finger salute, while frantically rummaging through metal cases of vinyl, sticking some out from the rest by their corners, obviously planning his night. What a pro I thought.

"Hey, look!" Said Ray, first into the dressing room, "A fridge, and some beers, coke, water and WOW! Sandwiches!"

"No Rick," I said as he was about to take the clingfilm off. "God you CAN'T be hungry."

"They look okay," Rick said. "Look! Pastrami!"

"Later! We can have them when we've finished."

"Bollocks." Rick said. "These are for our break.

"There's food later remember?"

"We are shooting straight off if that's okay." Paul said.

"Yeah of course." I said," Don't blame you."

I hadn't noticed Rick's shopping bag tucked away under his chair. Smokescreen came in and said, "Hi, can we be on stage bang on nine. Some big knobs from Rank are in. They want to see what all the noise is about."

Told us to break a finger - his idea of a joke on 'the break a leg' saying, then he was off, followed by Rick, as l guess he was off to the bar. Siobhan must have been special; Rick was wanting more. We got changed, I could hear the venue filling up as the noise level rose.

Smokescreen increased his noise level too, and increased the tempo a little.

Suddenly, at 8. 30. "Thriller" exploded through the JBL's with, "YO! Good evening everyone. Have we got a night for you…" etc.

Every now and then "Duelling Pianos", followed by a roar from the crowd and, "Hillbillies on Fire" followed by a lesser roar, would filter through the walls. Then Rick returned.

"Come on man, get changed." I said.

"I'm ready." Said Rick, pointing at his chest with both of his index fingers.

"Won't you get too hot with a jacket on?" I asked

"Nah." he said, "Let's go."

"Some big rank knobs in tonight, Smokescreen gave us the heads up."

"Well bully for them." Rick said.

The stage was blacked out, but we could see the auditorium was packed. It was heaving. We could feel the heat, the smell of sweat and a concoction of every perfume and aftershave, available on the High Street. Red dots of light showed us where the pianos were.

Ray took his position, puffed his cheeks, and looked up as if to say "ready". Paul put on his bass, and shrugged his shoulders, letting the bass relax onto his custom-made strap. He was ready. Smokescreen put one finger up. Sign for the last song he'd play, a short one so as not to keep us waiting.

"Ladies and Gentlemen." he shouted lowering the level of the music as he spoke every word, "it's that time again!..."

A few more seconds to add expectation, anticipation, then,

An explosion of light onto the stage. Every colour you could imagine. Spiralling spots arcing round the ceiling, eventually settling on us. Two Super Trooper spotlights from either side of the back wall, crisscrossed each other. One on Rick, one on me. and smoke of course.

"THE DUELLING PIANOS".

Rick was already 3 feet in the air coming down on the beginning of 'Great balls of fire' Ray, Paul, and I, were right on it. As he landed, we all came in bang on time. We nailed it.

"You shake my nerves," sang, or screamed Rick, and we were off.

The crowd came straight in with us. Jumping up, trying to mimic Rick.

"Goodness gracious great balls of fire…"

Ray and Paul motored like a finally tuned Race Engine. I couldn't contain my smile. Rick jumped, and jived, raising his fist in the air, and giving the crowd their now customary two finger salute, (not the V sign,) and once again we were off on this incredible journey of rock and roll, such energy, such volume, such feeling, such mayhem, yes, but we were never out of control. Rick took his solo. A dazzling array of jazzy, blue notes, crushed notes, orgasmic notes, at a blistering pace, just ahead of the beat for even more effect, then he signalled to me to start. No second verse here then. Rick was going for it. I started my solo, only to have Rick 'Land' next to me and play rhythm piano on my keyboard. It was thundering along and after only one verse of the first song.

"All right mate?" Rick shouted

"Fucking hell!" I shouted back, knowing my mic was off.

Next, he was up on my piano, starting the audience clapping - on the correct beat of course.

"Come on!" He shouted, "Girls only can dance on the pianos."

I didn't know the public were allowed on the pianos, even though we had steps for us to get up on them. All of a sudden, a torrent of females were storming to the front, and up the steps onto the stage, and then onto the pianos. A flurry of security personnel stopped them, after so many had made it to the stage, gave a customary 'thumbs up', to the rest of the security staff, to reassure them it was under control, and no further help was needed. Rick was back at his piano. A few feet behind me. We were playing back to back. He sang and played his heart out, loving this new dimension he'd added to our act.

Then, I got an elbow in my back as I was soloing.

"Look! Look!" Rick shouted excitedly, "Some have no knickers on!"

I looked up, and sure enough at least one of the girls on my piano was not wearing underwear, and she sure wanted me to know.

"Nice beaver"! Came over the speakers, Rick was enjoying every minute.

The rest of the set thundered on. Girls came and went. Security keeping a close eye on the numbers. Occasionally a guy would make it onto Rick's piano, only for Rick to jump up and kick him off, giving the security staff a cutthroat sign at any male who made it through. They soon caught on and only females made it through after that. Ray puffed, and Paul bounced, in perfect time. We finished our set to Smokescreen's,

"Give it up for the Duelling Pianos. The Duelling Pianos everyone. They'll be back soon, meanwhile here's some Quo."

'Rocking all over the world' cranked up and the audience danced, raced to the bar, or to the toilet, which ever need was greatest. We took an ice-cold beer from our new fridge.

"Good on Gary for fixing this." I said.

"Yeah, Ta Chris. I thought you might have had something to do with this." Added Paul.

"Cheers." Rick said to everyone, more of a congratulatory 'Well done', than just cheers.

We sat back in our chairs, getting our breath back, and drying the sweat off our faces, when the door burst open and in came Gary. "Rocking all over the world" momentarily coming in with him."

"Fuck me!" He said, red-faced and sweating too.

"They loved it!" 'They', being Top Rank's top brass.

"Brilliant just brilliant." He enthused.

"Thanks for the beers Gaz." I said, "Want one?"

"Eh? Oh that, that was a pleasure. No thanks," he said. "We've got some big noises in from head office, that Ted's brown nosing, but I think they love it. Think there's going to be one hell of a meeting Monday morning."

"Great." I said. "Let's hope they go with it. It certainly works - as a concept I mean."

"I know! It's bonkers out there. The bar can't cope, they've pulled staff from other parts of the complex to help out."

"Yeah, well tell him we'd like a rise on Monday if you're at that meeting." Rick chipped in.

"And can we have our own rooms paid for by Rank, it ain't going to cost them that much." I added.

"I probably won't be there, but I'm having a drink with Craig on Monday night, and he'll fill me in. I'll let you know what goes down." Gary said. "Good luck for later, keep it up; its fab. And I'll see you later for the after party."

"Yeah see you bud." We all said.

Just before 11, Rick went into the dressing room toilet saying, "See you on stage. Start 'Whole Lotta Shakin', and I'll be right out."

He had his shopping bag with him.

Ray and Paul hadn't noticed the bag.

Probably come out in a gorilla outfit I thought. That should be fun, but I couldn't shake off this heavy foreboding feeling that kept washing over me.

Rick was a pro; he wouldn't let me down. Rick didn't let me down.

What was in the bag certainly did.

The lights came up. I counted in 'A Whole Lotta Shaking,' and we started. A little calmer this time but rock solid and heavy. I had my back to the stage door, when I felt Rick's presence behind me, and I heard it too, as he joined in with us, adding more colour to the riff and groove we had going. Nothing from the audience to announce that a gorilla had appeared behind me. I was too curious, so I turned around. Nothing. Just Rick in a sleeveless black T-shirt. Moving in time, then he nodded to Ray and started the vocals. What was in that bag? I thought. He'd brought it with him, so it was obviously for tonight, and it was from the joke shop.

We went through the set; girls came and went. Rick jumped and jived and screamed away at every song.

Penultimate song now, maybe an encore or two and all going swimmingly well. We were racing through 'She Was Just Seventeen', I was singing this one, the last song, when I became aware of the audience pointing at something going on behind me, nudging the person next to them, and pointing harder, mouths open, some in hysterics, some in disbelief. I turned around and couldn't see Rick at the keyboard but looking up, I saw he was on the piano, having full-blown sex with a woman. Well I thought it was a woman, but then realized it was a blow-up, plastic doll with all the bells and whistles if you know what I mean. The big exaggerated open mouth for oral, I guess. And red lips, big boobs and all. He was 'doing her' – 'doggie style.' It was comical, as he pushed her down away from him 'she' kept springing back up. He might have got away with it had it not been for the fact he wasn't simulating anything; he had his erect todger out and was having full blown intercourse.

"Rick! Get down! Now!"

Ray puffed, and his eyes nearly popped out. At first glance it looked like a real woman.

Paul bounced and rolled his eyes.

"Rick, for fuck's sake"!

Rick ignored me, and turned 'her' around for oral sex. It looked a bit grotesque. I jumped up and snatched her from him and did a 'goalkeeper' style kick out into the back of the stage. 'She' went flying, and the crowd cheered and clapped and shouted, "More! More! More!" Ray and Paul had actually finished the song. There was silence for a long second as Smokescreen, who looked on in disbelief, shouted....

"ER THE DUELLING PIANOS EVERYONE," and quickly lined up the next song.

We scampered into the dressing room to the sounds of "More, more, more."

Rick was last in, giving his plastic friend a Fireman's lift into the dressing room. He was in hysterics; he couldn't contain himself.

"Rick, what the fuck?" I shouted.

"Eh?" Rick spluttered. "It was awesome, I had them going for a minute…!"

"That was mad. You could get us the sack."

"Bollocks. Rank won't part with us, and I'll promise not to do it again. Sorry, but it was funny. Come on man! Lighten up!"

I was expecting the door to burst open and half of Rank to come storming in. Smokescreen was first.

"Jesus! I've seen it all now!"

"Wasn't it sick?" Rick said, still busting a gut.

"Was weird," said Smokescreen", but funny too, you mad fucker"

Gary was next, followed by Craig, tripping over Gary's heels.

"Oh no, is it bad?" I asked.

"Er, not sure." Said Gary looking at Rick, like he wanted to kill him.

"Oh, come on man, it was a gas. They will be talking about this over their drinks for ages." Said Rick.

"Well that's the first time I've seen Ted take notice of anything on stage other than the Hillbillies," said Craig. "I think you might get away with it. Had it been a real woman though, it might have been very different."

"The crowd loved it," Said Rick, "listen, they're still shouting."

"Yeah it's been a riot." Said Craig. "I'll find out Monday if we're all in for a bollocking, or a rise." He added, "See you later at the party, you mad fucker."

"Yes, you little fucker." I said to Rick.
He just winked and deflated his 'friend'.

"And I thought you'd bought a gorilla suit." I said.
"Now there's an idea." said Rick "Why didn't I think of that!"
Oh no, I thought.

"When I first blew her up in the shop," Rick said,
"She had a willie!"

"A willie?" I asked.

"Yeah. then the shop assistant said I'd blown it up inside out!! Haaaarrrrgggghhhh, hah! Get it? Inside out! The fanny__"

"I got it. I got it!" I stopped him. "Very funny. Hah hah." I added, sarcastically.

Ray and Paul were shaking their heads as they got changed. Ray collected his snare drum and Paul his beloved Fender bass. They packed their stuff and said, "See you next week. "Let us know how the meeting goes."

"Okay guys," I said, "and thanks for this weekend. We couldn't have done it without you."

We all bear hugged and they left.

"You sick fuck." I turned to Rick

Rick, trying to suppress a smile, but not doing a very good job of it said; "Oh come on man. It was hilarious. No harm done. Bet it looked real from the audience's view."

"I think some of them did think that, judging by their reaction."

"I am off to see what's occurring at the bar. Coming?"

"See you in a bit." A tight bear hug, and Rick was gone. Phew! Nearly silence in the dressing room, just the booming bass coming through the walls. I still had that foreboding feeling and I looked at Rick's sex doll all deflated and distorted "Know just how you feel." I said to it. God, I was even talking to it now. I found Rick flaunting over Siobhan who immediately handed me a Becks.

"Thanks babe." I said and kicked Rick up the arse, as hard as I could.

"Hey! Not so hard!" He spluttered, on his Becks.

"Tell him how funny it was, Siobhan."

"It was funny Chris. We couldn't believe our eyes. I thought "That's it with him." Nodding at Rick. "Then I saw he was faking it. Priceless!!"

"He wasn't faking it!" I said.

"Oh Ricky, what you like?"

Then she was off, serving more drinks to more drunks. 1am. The bar finally closed. Security doing a great job, herding everybody out.

"Great guys!" we were getting back slapped by nearly everyone that passed us. Rick was getting his arse pinched and loving every minute of it.

"What about Son?" I asked.

"Ssshhhhhh, not now. "She's okay, I guess. Probably playing with her pink fluffy handcuffs I bought her."

"Handcuffs? How come that doesn't surprise me?"

"She loves them. I mean Handcuffed, well foot-cuffed too, we have four sets,"

How come that didn't surprise me either?

"I handcuffed her one night," Rick glugged his Becks, "and went down the pub."

"You WHAT?"

"Just a quick one. Man, she was gagging for it when I got back."

"God Rick, there is no stopping you. Please take it easy tonight. I need to sleep."

The after party was a bit lame. Everybody was too knackered. I signalled to Rick I was off, and he gave me a thumbs up and a wink.

I fell fast asleep and vaguely remembered Rick coming in. You know what it's like when someone is trying to be quiet, they are often noisier. He brought Siobhan and her friend back with him, and 'her,' Miss Plastic Doll.
I remember curling up in the duvet, and that was it.

I was out.

Chapter 11

"Come on tiger." Yvonne was waking Ed.

"Hi mum." he said, rubbing his eyes.

"Come on we going to surprise Daddy!"

"Oh yeah." Ed Suddenly sprang into life and jumped out of bed.

"Quick, wash, get dressed, and come down for porridge".

"Okay Mum. Yay!" Shouted Ed excitedly, "Can't wait to see Dad."

"That was quick, are you sure you washed?"

"Yeah, look!" He said, holding out his hands.

"Ok." Yvonne said, not looking. She poured out the porridge, extra milk for Ed, so it wouldn't be too hot.

"You got the presents and all the food?" Asked Ed.

"Yep, been up since six making pancakes. Can't you smell 'em?"

"Always smells of pancakes here Mum!"

Oh, that must be so nice for him she thought.

They finished their porridge. Yvonne finished her coffee, put the dishes into the sink to soak, and said to Ed, "Ready? Got everything?"

"Yep. Got Dad's card, can't wait to give it to him, he's gonna love it, isn't he Mum?"

"He certainly will. Come on let's go. Can you bring the Thermos and I'll grab the rest?"

"Yep got it! Why is it called a Thermos, mum?"

"Don't know. Maybe a Mr. Thermos invented them."

"Like Mr. Hoover?"

"Yeah I suppose so." Answered Yvonne.

It was a crisp autumn morning, as Yvonne eased the Volvo onto the A23 and headed for Brighton.

Rick had obviously had his all with the two girls and all three were half under and half out of the duvet. Miss plastic had, unknowingly to me, being placed behind me, and it looked like we were spooning. Rick had forgotten to close the door, but it was a quiet night, and very late, so no one, if anyone that is, noticed anything.

Yvonne turned to Ed and said, "Look out for 'The Regent Hotel', It's along here somewhere. Should notice it. It's a very big old building."

"There it is Mum!" Ed Shouted out, "up ahead, on the other side."

"That's it. Well done, should be easy to park, it being a Sunday."

Yvonne parked opposite the hotel. They entered through the glass doors and into the reception area. No one was behind the desk. It was mid breakfast, so the lobby was quite deserted.

"Daddy was right, it HAS seen better days." Yvonne said to Ed.

"Come on, we'll take the stairs, it's only one flight." Ed scooted on ahead, the excitement too much for him.

"Hang on!" Yvonne said. "They're probably still fast asleep, they had a late night remember?"

"What number Mum?"

"112." Yvonne answered.

"There it is!" Shouted Ed.

"Wait darling."

Ed shot ahead.

"Happy birthday Dad… Daaaaaaaaad, NO…"
Ed screamed, dropped the thermos and his card, and bolted past Yvonne, who'd just arrived at the open door to see what Ed had just seen. Rick on one bed, with two naked women, me now shrugging off Miss plastic, after being woken by Ed's screams.

"You fucking shit." Spat Yvonne, then, "Ed, wait Ed, Ed come back. Ed……"

"Fucking hell…" I put on some jeans and took off after them. Oh no. I was cursing Rick. Why couldn't he have fucking behaved just this once. God, what must that have looked like I thought.

Ed was out of the doors, with Yvonne after him, frantically screaming "STOP. ED. STOP."

The driver of the number 31 bus had no chance. Ed was in front of him, out of nowhere. Before he could even react, Ed bounced off the front of the bus and flew a metre or so through the air, landing motionless on the concrete road. The driver managed to stop the bus a few feet short of Ed. Yvonne saw it all, almost in slow motion, she tried to get to Ed before the bus. She'd have gone in front of the bus herself to push Ed out of the way, but she was too late. She was so close she ran into the side of the bus. This sent her sprawling, but she was up on her feet in seconds.

"ED, ED, no, no, please god no….." she screamed.

"Get an ambulance. Someone get a fucking ambulance. NOW!"

"Ed, Ed. Look at me. Please darling, open your eyes. Ed, please."

As I caught up with them, I shouted, "Don't move him. Yvonne don't move him."

"You fucking shit. Get away from me, don't touch me you dirty bastard. How could you? How fucking could you?"

"Yvonne, it wasn't__"

"Leave us alone…… get away from me."

We both looked at Ed. He started moving slowly. His face was gashed, where he'd hit the ground and slid along the rough concrete. He looked at me and I will never forget to this day that look of hate, pain, incomprehension, he gave me. He looked at his mum, and the state she was in scared the life out of him.

"Sorry mum." Ed said. "Forgot to stop at the kerb." he spluttered.

"It's alright darling. Where does it hurt?"

"Everywhere." Ed said, "I can't feel my legs."

"Oh God no, not that, please God, no please." pleaded Yvonne.

"Has someone called for an ambulance?" Yvonne screamed.

"It's on its way." came a voice from nowhere.

"Ed, keep still, don't try to move." I said.
Yvonne was taking off her cardigan and putting it over Ed.

"Don't move him." l said.

"I know. I'm a fucking nurse remember? How could you do that?? How long has it THAT been happening? Eh? Eh? We were so excited to surprise you, but what a fucking surprise we got didn't we? How could you?"

"It's not what it looked like." I said.

"Looked pretty obvious to me what it looked like." She spat out every word.

A small group of onlookers gathered round.

"Give us some fucking room." She screamed at the crowd.

I remember thinking I'd never heard Yvonne swear, ever.

"Where's that ambulance? Ed are you okay dear? Hang on, help is coming. We'll soon have you fixed up in no time."

"I'm cold mum." he said.

"Stay with us Ed. Stay with us. Help is coming any minute now".

Rick burst through the onlookers, almost falling on us. He only had jeans on too.

"No, No, Oh shit. I'm sorry what happened?"
Rick looked at the bus, then Ed, then said, "No. Jesus fucking Christ no... Is he okay? Shit, shit, shit."

"You mad, sick bastard. What were you two thinking of?" Demanded Yvonne.

"Yvonne, he wasn't doing anything. It was only me. It's only ever me" Rick said. "I can explain__"

"Fuck off Rick. This is too much right now, even you can't explain your sick way out of this..."
Sirens started getting closer.

"Out of the way!" I shouted, "Let the ambulance through."

"Chris, I'm sorry. I'm so sorry, oh fuck no, not Ed, please no." Rick was pacing around throwing his arms about.

"Keep it together Rick. I'm sure he'll be okay. He's a tough little bugger."

His legs worried me. No not this please God no.... I felt sick in my stomach, my mouth was as dry as hell. Yvonne kept looking at me with such disgust, such a hate. I'll never be able to mend this I thought and Ed, my beautiful little Ed, he didn't deserve this. Why didn't this happen to me? Not my precious Ed.

"What happened?" Asked the first paramedic, who jumped out of the ambulance, before it had even stopped.

"He was hit by the bus." Yvonne said. "He kind of bounced off it, and was airborne for a while, and landed right here. I haven't moved him, he's responsive, and conscious, feels cold, and says he can't feel his legs."

Yvonne was in nurse mode.

The second paramedic appeared with a large bright green bag, opened it and started taking everything out.

"That's probably just the shock." Said the first paramedic.

"What's your name little fella?" He asked Ed.

"It's__" I started.

Yvonne put out her hand palm up to stop me.

"Can you hear me son? What's your name?"

"Ed," came a little squeak.

"And what have you been up to hey?"

"I'm sorry." Whispered Ed, trying to look up at the ambulance man.

"That's okay." He said. "Not your fault. Can you tell me where it hurts?" He asked.

"Don't know." Ed answered.

The second paramedic had her stethoscope on Ed's chest.

"Can you breathe darling?" She asked Ed.

"I think so." Ed whispered.

"Sounds clear." She said to her partner, "And pulse is normal. Not racing. Maybe not too much trauma there."

"Does this hurt?" Asked the paramedic with the stethoscope as she gently pressed on Ed's chest.

"No, not really."

"This?" As she felt his legs.

"What?" Said Ed.

I was beginning to feel sicker by the minute. Just scoop him up and get into hospital I thought.

Ed tried to move and screamed out in pain.

"Don't. Stay dead still." Said the paramedic.

"Where did that hurt?" She asked.

"My leg." Ed said. "OW! OW! make it stop."

"Probably broken." she said to me, "and look it's very swollen."

"Neck brace." said the paramedic as she ran back to the ambulance.

"You a nurse?" Asked the first one.

"Yeah." said Yvonne. "Middlesex general."

"Ok. You can help us put on the neck brace. You know what to do, keep his head and neck as steady as you can. We'll put the brace on and get him on a scoop. We'll try to get him to A & E exactly as he is now. and they can take it from there.

"A scoop?" Rick asked, almost hysterically.

"It's okay." Said the paramedic, trying to reassure Rick. "It's just a bit of equipment to keep him steady. Any movement could be serious."

Another paramedic arrived on a motorbike.

"Can you see to the bus driver, Andy?" Asked the first paramedic.

"Sure. You're all good here?"

"Yep. Will get him on his way soon. He is stable enough. The bus hit him; the driver might be in shock."

"I'm on it." said the motorcycle paramedic and took off one of the bright green panniers from his motorbike and headed towards the bus.

The police arrived in a fanfare of sirens.

"Anyone see what happened?" The officer asked anyone, but soon gathered that Yvonne was his mum. Then a fire engine arrived. I wish Ed could have seen it all. He was looking but looked very blank.

He wouldn't look at me at all.

Yvonne explain to the police officer what she had seen, as she helped carefully fit Ed's brace around his neck.

"It wasn't the bus driver's fault" She said. "Ed just ran out straight in front of him." she added.

"Was he speeding?" Asked the officer.

"No. I don't know, I wasn't looking, I was trying to stop my son running out in front of the bus."

"Oh, the bus hit her too." someone said.

"Really?" Said the paramedic, "You okay?"

"Yeah, sure, it was nothing." Understated Yvonne. "Just a graze."

The paramedics looked at the 'scrape' on Yvonne's face then said,

"Let me look at your eyes."

"I'm ok, honest. Let's get him sorted."

The special stretcher arrived. It could split down its length. The two pieces were placed under Ed and then gently closed together, underneath him, kind of scooping him up without actually moving him. Now they could place him onto the mobile stretcher and lift him up into the ambulance, exactly as he had landed. The second paramedic was gently wrapping thick blankets around him, to keep him warm, and to stop any shivering from shock.

"On three." said the paramedic and they gently lifted Ed into the ambulance.

"You can come with us," he said to Yvonne, "you his dad?" To me.

"Yes".

"We are taking him to Brighton General. You can see it over there. He'll be in A&E for a bit. Are you ok?"

"Yeah sure." I said. "And thanks so much for helping Ed."

"That's ok. We better get going."

The ambulance drove off very slowly, with my precious family onboard, a quick burst of the sirens was probably a request from Ed.

"Come on Rick. To the hospital. You've got some serious explaining to do to Yvonne."

"Jesus. Sorry mate, I really am. Why didn't you tell me they were coming? I never would have__ "

"I didn't KNOW they were coming! I'd have booked me own room if I had."

"Can we go?" I asked the officer.

"Did you see what happened?"

"No, but my wife did. Can you ask her down at the hospital? I just have to see if he's okay."

"Yeah, sure off you go. I'll finish up here and be right down."

"Thanks mate."

I stuck my head inside the bus,

"You all right?" I asked the driver who was being breathalysed by the police officer.

"God, I'm so sorry." He said. "You his dad? I'm really so sorry, he came out of nowhere; he was so fast."

"Wasn't your fault." I said. "Don't blame yourself."

"Sorry." He kept saying. "Sorry."

"Come on Rick. Let's go."

Rick and I followed the signs to A&E. Yvonne wasn't in the waiting room. I asked at reception where my wife and son were.

"Edward?" She asked.

"Yes. He was knocked down by a bus. He came in with my wife not so long ago".

She looked through some cardexs and said,

"He's in thc Trauma unit right now. We'll know how he is soon. Just take a seat and I'll let you know as soon as I get more info." She said very professionally, with an equally professional smile.

We took a seat and Yvonne came in.

"You've got some fucking explaining to do." She whispered angrily. Some patients looked up from their magazines, then slumped back behind them.

"Yvonne, it's not what you think, honestly. You know I wouldn't do anything to hurt you and Ed."

"I know what I saw, and so did Ed. You freaked him out. He didn't know what to do. He just bolted past me. When I looked in the room I knew why. God what were you two up to? What were you doing? Don't lie to me please. I'd rather have the truth than you lying. Just tell me for fuck's sake."

"Yvonne." said Rick.

"Oh, this better be good Rick". She hissed.

"Yvonne, he's never, ever betrayed you, ever."

"Oh Rick. Please," she snarled.

"Yvonne. I mean it. You know he wouldn't do anything bad. You and Ed are his life."

"Do you often have orgies when you're out of sight?"

"We weren't having an orgy Yvonne, honest."

"What? Three women between you isn't an orgy? Does it have to be more before it's an 'orgy'? Rick, you're full of shit and you know it. Sonja might put up with this sort of behaviour, but believe me, I'm not."

"Yvonne, Chris has never cheated on you. He wouldn't. What you saw was a blow-up doll I got from the joke shop for last night's show. I put it in bed with

Chris for a joke so when he woke up, he'd get a fright. I was with two bar staff I know. Chris was asleep when we got back, so I just crept in. I was really pissed anyway. Chris has never, ever, participated in anything at any time, I swear."

"What? You normally bring back women? What will Sonja think?"

"She knows, I tell her."

"What? And she's ok with that? Jeez. I must have a word with her."

"And you.." she turned to me. "This happens often? You said he comes back with a woman sometimes. I tried not to think about it, thought you were joking, exaggerating to boost Rick's reputation, I honestly believed nothing was happening every time you're away. Jesus."

"Yvonne, it doesn't. Occasionally he brings someone back and I just turn the other way and hide under the duvet. I had no idea what was going on last night, and I promise you I have never, never, ever, ever, laid a finger on anyone since I met you. You've got to believe that Yvonne, please."

I took her hand there was no squeeze back, no hug, she was in tears, and completely broken.

"I have to think about this. Ed better be okay or you…..," pointing to Rick, "have got a lot to answer for. A blowup doll? What for? I daren't even go there."

"Er..." he was doing something on the piano with her, he thought it was funny, I took it off him and kicked it off stage.

"Oh, I bet Rank loved that." She said. "You've probably lost your job now. What were you thinking Rick? What were you doing?"

"Yvonne, I'm sorry. I never thought this would happen. Honest. I love Ed, I'm so sorry. It's my fault. I didn't know you were coming down; I have gotten another room; I'd have gone back to theirs. I promise I would."

"Well it's separate fucking rooms from now on."

"Yvonne. I'm sorry, I really am."

"A blowup doll!?" She said to me.

"Yes." I said. "You have to believe me, and I didn't even know it was there, honestly, I didn't. I would never hurt you. You must know that. I'd never jeopardize what we have. You and Ed are everything to me. Please Yvonne, I've never touched anyone ever."

"Fucking hell. What a mess. I'll never forgive you for this Rick. Ed bad better be okay. Or...." Yvonne ran out of things to say, she was so angry.

"I'll get some water." Rick said. Pointing at the water cooler and wanting some space.

I gave Yvonne a hug and pulled her close to me. This time she relaxed a little, but was convulsing with shock and tears.

"Poor little Ed." she sobbed. "Poor Ed. God, I hope he's ok. I can't believe this, it's like a nightmare. I just want to wake up and everything will be okay. He was so excited to see you, and surprise you. So was I. You should have seen his face when we spotted the hotel. He could hardly contain himself. That's why he got to your room first. There was no stopping him. He'd made you a card and was so proud of himself when he brought it home."

"I'm so sorry Yvonne. I never thought in my wildest dreams anything like this would happen. It was really nice of you to do all that. You know how much I hated to be away on one of our special days. We'll have more special days won't we Yvonne? I haven't done anything, ever, I promise you sweetheart. It's just so unbelievable. I can't get my head round it. God how is Ed? Can't they at least let us see him, be with him? He's probably frightened."

"They'll let us know as soon as they know, I'm sure. He'll be in trauma, getting everything checked. Oh God he's probably in theatres now." Yvonne was shaking. Rick came back with the water, looking terrified and sat back down, not sure whether to speak or not.

"I'm just going to find a loo." he said. More about giving us space then needing to go.

"Come here." I said to Yvonne. "Let me hold you please."

"I'm sorry I doubted you." She said, finally holding me and squeezing me.

"Shhhh, it's okay. I can't blame you. It must've been a shocking sight. Can't help thinking what's going through little Ed's mind. Poor little thing".

"We'll just blame Rick." Yvonne said, meaning it.

"Don't know how we explain what a plastic doll is for. We'll just say Rick was playing a joke on you."

"Crickey. How do we do that? And he saw real women on Rick's bed. They weren't exactly covered up. Fuck". Yvonne swore. "What must he be thinking?"

"I just hope he's okay. I hope he knows it wasn't me doing anything bad. "We could get Rick to explain he thought it would be funny for me to wake up and get a shock."

"Not sure I want Rick explaining anything to Ed." She said.

"Yeah but if it comes from him, Ed will still see me as his hero. God I'd hate to lose that. To lose him."

"You won't. We'll always love you. Ed will understand and probably go off Rick for a while, as long as he knows we are okay, he'll be fine!"

"Hope he is fine. How long do these things take?"

"Don't know. Depends on the injuries. God, I hope he's not badly hurt. It was horrible seeing it all. I was screaming for him to stop. I just couldn't catch him; he was really moving. I could see the bus, and Ed, and I just thought NO! NO! I was so helpless. Then when he went flying, I couldn't breathe. I remember hitting the bus, and falling over but I just had to get to Ed. I had to tell him his mummy was here and not to be frightened. It was horrific."

"I know. I came out and you were kneeling over him, my heart nearly burst. Fuck……. Come on hurry up."

A tri-age nurse stuck her head out of the door and signalled us to come in.

"Oh God, how is he?" Yvonne asked before we made it to the door.

"Sit down." She said. "Ed's going to be fine."

"Oh God, thank you God." Yvonne said, looking up to heaven. I took her hand and held it tight.

The nurse was putting up some x-rays on one of those backlit panels. They just looked like negatives to me.

"Shit." Said Yvonne, obviously used to seeing these kinds of images, and knowing already Ed's injuries.

"It's not that serious," the nurse said.

"Well I can see two broken ribs and a broken humerus already." Yvonne said.

I was suddenly so proud of her.

"Ok. Slowdown said the nurse. We think the bus hit him side on."

"It did." Yvonne said.

"Hence the broken arm, and the two broken ribs, caused by the arm colliding with them."

"What else?" Yvonne asked.

"Nothing internal, we can see so far. He has a bad gash on his face. Shouldn't leave much of a scar. We'd like to keep him in for a couple of days, just for obs. If his vitals are normal you can take him home. You're a nurse?" She asked Yvonne.

"Yes. Trauma and orthopaedics. Middlesex central."

"Thought so." The nurse said." You know how to read an x-ray. You can probably take him home as soon as the consultant is happy he is stable. I'll let him know his mother is a trained nurse and he'd be happy to know Ed is in good hands."

"Can we see him?" I asked.

"Yes sure, he's a bit out of it at the moment, and groggy from the anesthetic."

"Anesthetic?" Yvonne asked.

"Yes, we thought it better to put him under. His arm had to be reset. It was only for a few minutes. That way he didn't feel anything, and now he's on a saline drip with paracetamol. He might need something stronger when he wakes up."

"I don't think so." said Yvonne, seemingly annoyed she wasn't asked if he could have an anesthetic.

"Follow me, I'll take you to him. His face is very swollen so be prepared. But honestly, we are all happy with him. He is going to be fine."
She took Yvonne's arm and led her out of the door.
I followed, preparing myself.

Ed was lying very still. Asleep probably. He had a big white bandage diagonally over his face. His arm in a plaster, but not in a sling and a big plaster cast over his chest, probably for keeping the ribs stable until they had healed, I thought.

"Oh Ed, Ed, its mummy. Are you okay darling?" Ed didn't move.

"We are bringing him round." Said the nurse caring for him. "He was awake and talking in recovery; asking for his Mum. Yvonne is it?"

"Yes. I'm his mum."

"He was asking for you. I said you'd be along in a minute. He slips in and out of sleep. Should be ok in a few minutes". She reassured us. She left us alone with him, asking us to press the button if we needed anything. We thanked her and rushed to Ed's side.

"Give me that squash." Yvonne instructed. "There, with a straw in it". I passed it to her, she had gone straight into nurse mode. Checking the screen linked up to him. His heartbeat looked normal to me. The rest was just gobbledygook.

"Oh, look at his face." She said.
It was very swollen, his eye outside of the bandage looked so swollen, I thought he'd never be able to open it. God knows what the other one was like.

"That where the gash is?" I asked Yvonne, pointing at the bandaged part of its face.

"Yes. Shit, I hope it doesn't leave him disfigured."

"The nurse said it shouldn't cause too many problems."

"Comc on." Yvonne whispered close up to him.
Ed's eye flicked and opened for a second.

"Ed, it's Mummy and Daddy," she said.
Ed opened his eye, and looked at his Mum.

"You're going to be fine darling." Yvonne said.

"S... S... Sorry Mum." He forced out. "What, was... Was..."

"Shhhh." Yvonne said. "Take it easy. Here, sip some of this."

Ed sucked a bit on the straw. Obviously dying for a drink, but it must've been too painful for him, he pulled away quickly.

"What was... was... Dad doing?" He slurred out.

"It's okay darling. Rick was playing a joke on him, and it all went wrong Daddy was asleep and didn't know anything about it."

"But." a pause and then "but__"

"Not now darling, everything is alright. Daddy hasn't done anything wrong. You just get better and all will be fine soon. I promise you, sweetie, it's all okay.
Ed was trying to open his eye, more to see Yvonne.

He didn't look at me.

"How long do you think they'll keep him in?" I asked.

"Probably overnight for obs."

"I should go and book us a room."

"Ok. Give me a bit of time with Ed. I'll make sure he gets everything he needs, and I'm here when he wakes up properly. Come back soon."

"Yeah sure."

"I'll try to explain everything to him. I'm sure it will be okay. Go on."

"Ok, and Yvonne, I'm so sorry."

"I know. It's okay. Go on, see you later."

Yvonne was in total nurse professional mode and began sorting Ed out. Fiddling with drips and lines and checking his monitor. I gave Yvonne a hug and kissed Ed on the forehead. My heart was breaking. Poor Ed, he didn't deserve this, nor did Yvonne. Rick was waiting outside in the waiting room. He looked awful, partly from drink and lack of sleep, but also terrified at what had happened to Ed. He jumped out of his seat when he saw me.

"How is he? Chris, I'm so, so, sorry, I didn't mean this to happen…"

"It's okay." We bear hugged, then. "Come on, let's get out of here." l said.

We walked out of the hospital and headed back to the hotel.

"He's got a broken arm and two broken ribs."

"Shit. Shit." Said Rick, trying to keep up with me as I was marching along in angry mode.

"He's going to be ok." I said, calming an agitated, scared, Rick. "He's got bruising to his face, nothing life changing, he was very lucky. God we've been so lucky."

"Jesus. I'm so sorry man, I really am, I had no idea."

"Rick, it's okay."

"But it's all my fault."

"No, it's not, you didn't, I didn't know they were coming, it couldn't be helped.

"Fuck me, and that was supposed to be your birthday surprise. Shit. What a fuck up."

"It's done now. I need a coffee and I've got to stay tonight. You alright on the train?"

"Eh? Yeah, Oh yeah, of course. Son is going to be mortified and she WILL blame me. I know it."

"Just say we were all totally blasted, and you can't remember much, and the plastic doll was a joke you played on me, that went terribly wrong. She'll understand."

"Hope so. She'll never forgive me for hurting Ed, she loves him."

"I know, and I know you do, but he's going to be okay."

"Maybe he'll hate me now." Rick said head down.

"No. We'll explain everything to him and I'm sure in time it will be okay. We need to sort out our room and check out." I said, as we approached the hotel entrance. We entered the hotel, and the receptionist who had checked us in Thursday, came running over.

"Oh my God. Is everything okay? I heard what happened."

"Yes, not too bad." I said, "My son is going to be fine he was very lucky."

"Oh, thank God, if there's anything I can do."

"Thank you. I will need another room for tonight."

"Sure. I can fix that."

Upstairs the door was still open, the beds were a mess. My birthday treat had been placed on one of the beds. The girls had disappeared. Miss plastic was sitting up against the wall.

"Jeez." Rick said, "What a mess." He deflated miss plastic, and tried to stuff her in the waste bin, giving up leaving her rear sticking out.

"Rick, please," I said nodding at the unsightly waste bin.

"Bollocks to it." He said, and just kicked it over.
We grabbed our things and went back to reception. The receptionist had a key already, to hand to me.

"On the house." she said. "We are so sorry. Hope you're both going to be ok." she said.

"Oh this?" I said nodding at the key, "Is for me and my wife, we have to stay over tonight, so could I have a double please?"
I guessed she thought it was for me and Rick and therefore gave us a twin.
I definitely needed a double tonight.

"Oh! Yes of course, no problem," and she took the key, and busied herself behind the desk.

"Here you are, 416." she said. "Enjoy."

"Thank you."

I took the key and headed outside.

"I'll put all the stuff in the car." I said to Rick. "Anything you want me to take?"

"Just my case, if that's okay. I can take the rest."

"Sure. Stick it in. Come on let's find a coffee. There is a train every hour, so phone Son, and let her know what happened, and when you'll be back okay?"

"Yeah sure, okay mate, sorry again."

The cortado hit the spot. Rick looked defeated, deflated, like Miss plastic, and there was fear in his eyes. I've never seen Rick like this before. He really did have a heart.

"You're going to have to tell Son everything." I said.

"Yeah I know. Shit what a mess. She'll be furious with me. Not so much for the other women, but for hurting Ed, and you both of course".

"Well I wouldn't leave anything out because she's bound to talk to Yvonne, and she'll just tell it as it was. Don't lie to her on this one it'll only make it worse."

"I know. Oh God I'm dreading going home."

"Well you have to do, and ring her before you leave. Explain what happened, and why you're taking the train, might soften it when you get back."

"Yeah, you're probably right. Are you going to the hospital now?"

"Yes, thought I'd take in my breakfast treat and try to salvage some of it. God knows what's going through his mind now. I'm sure Yvonne will be trying to put it right, saying it was a prank that went terribly wrong, and I didn't really know anything about it. That way, in Ed's mind, I haven't committed any crime. So hopefully it will be ok."

"God. Please tell them both I am so sorry. That I never meant to hurt them. Ed's never going to like me again after this."

"Well you may have to square that with him. Hopefully in time maybe."

We finished our coffees, bearhugged and said our goodbyes.

"Good luck mate." Were Rick's parting words.

Chapter 12

I grabbed Yvonne's bag of birthday treats, and put it on my shoulder, picked up the Thermos, and saw Ed's card. Just a folded piece of paper. I didn't want to open it until I was with Ed. I would give it to Yvonne, to give to Ed, who'd give it to me. I hoped. I started to well up and feel sick. How exciting it must've been for them both; getting up really early and preparing my treat. Ed would have loved that, and it was all, nearly, destroyed in seconds.

The hospital was quiet, being a Sunday. I headed for the High Dependency Unit, where Ed would still be, I presumed. No hustle bustle today, just a few visitors carrying takeaway coffees, and magazines to their loved ones, unfortunate enough to be in here. Someone with a stethoscope hurried past, obviously covering a lot today, being a skeleton staff, I suspect. I found Ed and Yvonne where I had left them. The nurse nodded with a professional smile, to go in, I'd seen Yvonne use those smiles when we were out together. Nothing flustered her. Just gave out that beautiful smile and carried on. Nothing flustered Yvonne, not even being hit by a bus. She got up immediately and tended to Ed. It must've been really painful, as I looked at her bruises all down her right side, in bed later that night. She was much stronger than me.

"Hi buddy." I said to Ed, and gave Yvonne a kiss, which seemed welcomed. She didn't turn away.

"You alright.?" She asked.

"Kind of", I said, "how is he?"

I walked around to the other side of the bed and give Ed a kiss on the forehead.

"He's fine." Said Yvonne.

"You okay mate?" I asked Ed.

"Yeah, think so Dad."

At least he was still calling me Dad.

"Ed I'm really sorry…"

Yvonne put her arm palm up as if to say, 'not now'.

"Dad? What was Ricky doing?"

"He got drunk and brought some friends back and they all crashed in his bed." I explained. "I had no idea they were there. I was out for the count when they came back. It must've been very late.

"But dad, Ricky was with other women and I thought you were too. I__"

"Ed, I'd never be with another woman. I love Mummy, and you, too much, to do anything like that."

"Stupid Rick, put a pretend woman in your bed?!"

"Yes!" I said. Ed was even starting to see a funny side.

Yvonne wasn't. I couldn't.

"But why have a pretend woman Dad? Where did Rick get that from?"

I immediately seized on the 'joke' side of things.

"He bought it in a joke shop. He wanted to dance with it on the piano. He thought it would've been very funny."

"Oh, was it dad?"

"No. I kicked his arse for__"

"Chris!" Yvonne hissed.

"For being so stupid." I finished.

"Hah! Ouch!" Said Ed, as the laugh had obviously hurt his face.

"Sorry Ed. So sorry."

"I've brought that lovely birthday breakfast you and Mum made, shall we have it now?"

"Chris, he can't eat anything. Look at him!"

He was very bruised and swollen. I'm sure it was hurting Yvonne and I, even more.

"Oh yeah, happy birthday Dad. Mum have you got Dad's card?"

"Yes, here it is darling, he made it all himself."

I'm sure Ed was beaming under the swelling.

Yvonne put Ed's card into his good hand, and he passed it to me.

"Wow! What's this?" I enthused.

I opened the folded piece of paper to reveal an amazing drawing of a big red fire engine, with a man holding a little boy's hand. Me and him, I guess.

"Wow Ed. That's amazing! Is that me and you?"

"Yeah! Do you really like it Dad? Miss Barnes thought it was good. She gave me 10 out of 10."

"Not surprised." I said. "It's brilliant. Thank you matey."

I leaned over and kissed him on his forehead. He was smiling this time, and put his good arm around my neck and held on.

"Love you Dad. Sorry I ran off when I saw__"

"It's okay Ed. I'm sorry you had to see that. It won't happen again; I've told Rick separate rooms from now on."

"Oh, but you and Rick like telling jokes to each other before you go to sleep, and you'll be all alone if you have your own room."

"Yeah, well it'll be safer eh? No plastic people and Rick's loud headphones."

"Yeah, can't believe he has music so loud in his headphones it keeps you awake Dad."

"Pancakes anyone?" Yvonne asked. "Don't know what they'll be like now, but we can see, and cold crispy bacon with maple syrup. Coffee might still be drinkable."

"Can I just have a pancake with syrup mum please?" Asked Ed, determined not to miss out.

"Of course, darling, are you sure you can manage it?"

"Yes, I think so, I'm starving."

That must be a good sign I thought.

We sat and had my birthday treat after all. Not what I was expecting, but it could have been so much worse. Thank God Ed was going to be alright. We stayed and chatted till 9pm, Ed drifting in and out of sleep. Then a nurse came in and said we'd have to leave, and that Ed was in good hands and would be well looked after with hourly Obs, due to his head injury. They weren't too concerned about him.

Yvonne tucked Ed in. I gave him a kiss on the forehead.

"Night Dad, don't worry I'll be ok, I promise."

"Goodbye," I said. "My little man, aren't you?"

"Yeah Dad, and sorry again."

"Shhh…. don't think about it, just get better quickly for me and Mummy."

"I will Dad. Night Mum."

"Night darling. Here is your button to press if you want anything or feeling painful or hungry. Anything. Ok?"

"Yeah thanks Mum. Love you. Love you Dad."

Thank God for that. He still loves me. He's not hating me, like I imagined he would.

"Bye sweetie." Yvonne said at the door.

"Bye matey." I said.

"Bye." Ed muttered, probably half asleep already. Yvonne stopped at the nurses station as we left. I waited by the swing doors to the ward. She was obviously discussing Ed, and asking what the plan was, leaving our contact numbers and so on. Finally, she said thanks to the nurses, and headed towards me.

"All good?" I asked.

"Yeah. Just making sure they know how to get hold of us, in case Ed starts fretting, but I'm sure he'll be okay."

"Come on let's get some sleep." I said.

"Where are we staying?"

"At the Regent. They gave us a room on the house after they heard what happened."

"That was nice of them. Rick?"

"He took the train home earlier."

"Wait till Son hears this one." She said.

"I wouldn't like to be Rick right now."

Rick got home, told Sonja everything and she was beside herself. Horrified at Rick but not surprised. She slapped him hard and wanted to get the first train to Brighton, but Rick managed to talk her out of it.

"What were you thinking?" She kept saying to Rick, pacing up-and-down, not knowing what to do with herself. Rick would apologise and apologise.

"A plastic blow-up doll? Eh?"

"It was for a joke on the piano." Rick would protest.

"And poor Ed saw all that? No wonder he freaked. God, I hope he's okay. I'll never forgive you if anything happens__

"He's going to be fine." Rick would say and try to calm Sonja down.

We got back to the Regent, found our room, showered, and went straight to bed. I held Yvonne in my arms as she lay on her back. She looked done in, but still so beautiful.

"I'm so sorry darling." l said.

"You better be."

I gave her a long kiss on the lips, and she didn't turn away.

That's because she was fast asleep.

Chapter 13

The next morning, we both bolted down a quick breakfast, and headed straight over to the hospital. We found Ed sitting up in his bed, tucking into porridge. His face lit up when he saw us, then he winced. He'd forgotten his injuries, and after what must've been eye watering pain, (I thought he was crying) that big, wide, Ed smile came back.

"Hi Mum, Hi Dad." He said excitedly.

"Hi darling." Yvonne said, leaning over to kiss him on his 'good' side."

"Hi matey." I said, and we fist bumped.

"You ok?" Yvonne asked.

"Yeah fine. I couldn't sleep so I watched a bit of telly. Look, it's right over the bed. Can I have one at home?"

"No, of course not!" Yvonne said, laughing out loud. A nurse appeared and introduced herself to us.
She had been on night duty and was coming in to say goodbye to Ed, and to check on him.

"He's been a very good boy." She said.

"No trouble at all, and so brave. Look at him, love him."

Ed was beaming. He loved praise. His good eye was wide open, and that big smile was still there. It took a lot to keep him down and even his injuries had not dampened his spirit. 'That's my boy', I thought, I was so proud of him.

"His obs have been very good all night." The nurse said to Yvonne.

"Yes, I've read his chart." Yvonne replied.

"Oh, are you a nurse?"

"Yes. Middlesex general."

"Oh great, then I'll leave you with him. I think he may be allowed out later. Mr. Rees will do his round about 11, so hang on and talk to him. If he knows Ed is going home to a professional, He'll have him out in no time. We need the beds!"

"Yes, tell me about that one." Yvonne sighed.

"Same up there?" Asked the nurse.

"Yes, we're always on black alert" (that's one short of closing the hospital completely)

"Hmmph. One day they'll sort out the NHS otherwise...... Okay, I'm off, good luck with Ed. Take care little fella, thanks for being my best patient ever!" Ed squirmed with pride then winced again.

"Is He still on paracetamol?" Asked Yvonne.

"Yes. Every four hours. I think his next one is at 12."

"Okay, thanks for looking after him.

"No probs. Bye then."

"Bye." I said.

"Bye." Yvonne said.

"Right young man." Yvonne sat by the bed face-to-face with Ed.

Ed looked scared, like he did when he thought he was in trouble. I went to sit on the bed. Mistake.

"NO! NO!" Yvonne retorted. "You never sit on the bed. Contamination. You might have been sitting on a park bench or a dirty bus seat, who knows!"

"Sorry." I said, jumping up, and at the same time, making a scared face to Ed. He laughed and winced again.

"Keep him calm!" Yvonne said. "Don't make him jump or laugh."

"Sorry, again."

"Right Edward," she said to him.

Now Ed knew she was going to say something very important. I always got 'Chris', but when it was 'Christopher', I knew it wasn't going to be good.

Ed paid attention, looking very serious.

"What you did wasn't anything wrong. None of this is your fault and you mustn't blame yourself." Yvonne told him. Ed visibly relaxed. Then winced again.

"That silly Rick," She continued, "did a stupid thing playing a joke on Daddy like that."

I could see Ed desperately trying to contain a smile.

"So, it's no wonder you turned and ran. I bet you thought it was a real woman. I did for a split second."

"I did Mum," Ed splurted out, "it was so real; I didn't know they made plastic women!! Who'd want one of them?"

"Rick thought it would be a blast," I said. "and was mucking about on top of the piano, dancing with it," (I couldn't bring myself to say "her") "and swinging it around his head. I wondered what the audience were pointing and laughing at."

"Wow!" said Ed, trying to picture it in his head.

"Must have been funny then. Silly Rick, putting it in your bed when you were asleep."

"I know. But you know what Rick is like. He put a firework in my bed once and tried to light it!"

"Ha! Ha! OW! Did he?"

"No just kidding."

"Daaad!

"Stop!" Yvonne said, "Don't wind him up. How many times……?"

"Sorry. Sorry. Won't do it again."

Ed didn't mention the two women in Rick's bed, so I let it go. I was so pleased he believed us and so relieved he wasn't angry with me. I felt a great weight lift off my shoulders and for the first time in hours felt relaxed and a bit more 'normal'.

"Right then We're good are we."

"Yes Mum, we are really good."

"Let's get you washed then."

"Aw mum!"

"And maybe Daddy can get some new clothes for you, to go over the plaster, something baggy and warm."

"A fireman's outfit!" Said Ed.

"How about a tracksuit?" I suggested.

"Ok," Ed said, a tad disappointed, "can I have a blue one?"

"You can have whatever you want, soldier."

"That's a good idea." Yvonne said.

Any praise from Yvonne right now was very much appreciated from me. I'd escaped a possible family meltdown, and it felt wonderful. Ed was going to be okay and his spirit and love were still intact. Thank God for that.

"Get two sizes up, a 7 to 9-year-old maybe."

"Ok, I'm on it. Back in a bit."

"See you Dad. Thanks."

I think Ed was excited at the prospect of a brand-new tracksuit. I left them to do their thing. I knew Yvonne would clean him up and get him sorted. I called Rick.

"Jesus man. How is he? How are you? Yvonne?"

"Calm down mate, we're all good here."

I heard Sonja, hysterical in the background shouting "How is he? Is he alright? Can we come down and help? Can we___?"

"Shhhhhh!" Said Rick! I'm trying to hear."

I gave Rick an update, I said we'd hoped to be back later, and I'd pop round for a chat if it wasn't too late.

"Yeah come round any time man. It would be great to see you."

"Okay see you later." As I hung up, I could hear Sonja frantically saying to Rick, "Well, how is he? what's......" and then they were both gone. Rick will be getting an ear bashing I thought, and he most definitely deserved one.

It was Sunday, so I wasn't sure what would be open. Some shops were closed, some open, for the weekenders, so it was the gift shops and the like. Oh, and my favourite coffee bar was open. Great.
I sat with my flat white and thought I'd better call Ray, and Paul, and gave them the lowdown. They were both horrified and sympathetic at the same time.

"I'm gonna chin that Rick". Ray had said.

"Don't worry, I think Sonja is doing that right now."

"Anything we can do, just shout". Paul had said, kindly. I said we'd regroup later in the week, and Friday at Hemel was still on. I finished my flat white and went tracksuit hunting. I soon found one in a sports shop. A royal blue one with some fancy designer logo on the left breast, that I knew wasn't a football team, and thought Ed would like it. He loved it. He wanted to wear it straight away, but Yvonne wouldn't let him. She told Ed he'd have to wait for the doctor to examine him. Ed looked disappointed and slumped back onto his bed and winced again. At 11 o'clock precisely, Mr. Rees appeared. He looked very dapper. A greying man wearing an immaculate dark blue suit and a blue and white polka dot tie. After the introductions, he looked at Ed's chart, then turned his attention to Ed's injuries.

"Well now!" He said to Ed, looking at his plastering. Ed looked scared. "You've been a very lucky chap." He said. "All this will be well healed in about six weeks." He said to us. "I think he can go because I hear you're a fully trained registered general nurse." 'Ward sister', or used to be I thought in my head. After Ed had arrived, Yvonne returned to work but wanted hands-on caring, not a bureaucratical job, sitting in the ward office, bogged down by paperwork.

"Yes, I can take care of him." She said.

"Okay. I'll sort it out with the discharge nurse, and you can get going."

"Thanks Mr. Rees," we both said.

"No problem. Take care little fella, and take it easy for a while. Complete rest from now on. Do what your Mum tells you", and after a glance at me, "and your Dad too, of course".

"Ok, I will doctor, I promise." Ed replied.

"Great." said Yvonne, after he was through the door.

"Let's get him dressed and see if he can sit on the chair. This is going to hurt, so I'll see if I can get something stronger, don't really want to, but they may have some Ibrufen, or a patch, or something like that."

"Ok." I said. Leave it to me. I'll be careful."

Yvonne left Ed to me. I thought that was very encouraging, and I set about gently taking off his gown. Then I thought I should wait for Yvonne to return with a stronger drug. She did and I got brownie points for waiting. She stuck a patch on Ed's back, just below the hairline and said we should wait a few minutes for it to kick in.

"Still going to hurt him." she whispered to me.

I started packing Ed's stuff away in the hospital bag. No point really, his old clothes had been cut off in theatre. We sat down for a while. Yvonne stroking Ed's forehead and he fell fast asleep.

"Poor thing must be exhausted." She said.

"Is that the patch working?" I asked.

"No, he's probably knackered from the anaesthetic, and all night telly."

"Yeah, I bet he'd love one of those in his bedroom."

"In his dreams." She said.

"Why don't we do it now, slowly and gently while he's dozing?"

"Not a bad idea." Yvonne said.

The brownie points were starting to add up.

"You gently take his gown off while I keep stroking his head. We might get away with it."

Gently, I took off Ed's gown, he twitched now and again but I managed it. More brownie points.

I managed to pull up the tracksuit bottoms, but would have to lift him, to get them up to his waist.

"If I lift him very slowly and gently could you pull up his tracksuit bottoms?" I asked Yvonne.

"Sure, let's try."

We managed that, and put his top on without waking him.

"Great." said Yvonne. "That's saved him a lot of angst."

The discharge nurse arrived with Ed's notes and discharge letter, and some meds.

"We'll get a porter to wheel him to your car. He may still be a bit groggy for a while.

"Ok, that's great." Yvonne said. "Thank you."

Ed stirred and noticed his tracksuit.

"Wow!" Followed by, "OW!" But then a big smile. I was so happy he liked it. It would take his mind off things I thought. We got Ed into the car gently and started our journey home. Very slow and labourious, but so happy he was okay. I held Yvonne's hand as we drove, and she gave me the odd squeeze now and again. I was smiling. So was Ed, in the mirror, then he was fast asleep. I speeded up a little, and soon we were home. Bliss.

I told Rick we'd speak tomorrow, and we would regroup in Gary's office at two. So, a coffee at one would be great. He agreed. I ran upstairs to find Ed asleep in his bed, tracksuit still on, but open so he didn't get too hot. Yvonne was running a bath, and as she got in, she said, "Joining me?"

I joined her. More bliss.

Chapter 14

Rick was already waiting for me at 'Aroma,' our favourite coffee house. The decor was coffee coloured, with hessian sacks of various coffee varieties, dotted around the place, leading you to believe they imported their own coffee. They were far too small to do that, of course, but the beans were roasted just up the road, and the coffee was fabulous.

The aroma hit me as soon as I entered, the barista nodded at me, I nodded back and went to sit with Rick. The coffee would arrive in minutes. Rick jumped up, for his customary bear hug. He looked like he had just done ten rounds with Sonja. Then he told me he had.

"Aw man, good to see you. I've been so worried and depressed, sick in my stomach. I haven't eaten, and Son's giving me the third degree."

"Don't worry mate, everyone's okay, that's the main thing."

"Shit, shit, and shit. I never meant anything like that to happen, especially not to Ed. You know I love him, and I'd kill anyone who hurt him I'd…"

"Rick, it's fine. I haven't got the arse with you. Guess it was funny really. Even Ed thinks it was."

"He DOES?? What? He's okay with this?"

"I had to explain it somehow. He thought he'd seen me with a real woman. When I told him it was a plastic one you use for dancing with on the piano, and then you put it in my bed for a joke, he could hardly contain himself."

"Wow. Thanks for that. I thought you three wouldn't see me again. How is he?"

"He's fine. He's a tough little bugger, gets it from Yvonne, Broken arm, broken ribs, gash to the face, nothing too serious there, but his spirit hasn't even been dented."

"Jesus! No! Poor little thing, and it's all my fault."

"Rick, it's ok, God, it could've been a lot worse."

"Yvonne?"

"Yeah, we're good. Sorry but you might be in for some flack, but it'll be ok. You will see."

"She thought__"

"Yep. She thought it was a real one too. She was so off me, I thought I could never repair this, and you with two real ones in yours. She thought we did that sort of thing all the time. Kept telling me to get away from her, it was horrible. Thought I'd blown everything."

"Well not you, me." Rick said.

"No, she didn't know it was a plastic doll, and she didn't know you'd planted it there, so obviously thought the worst".

"Fuck. Sorry man."

"Want another?" I asked.

"I'll get them." Rick started to get up.

"Nah, sit down."

I caught Jim, the barista's, eye and nodded with two fingers up.

"Coming up." He said.

"Son's gone over to yours to see how they both are, and ask if she can help. That alright?"

"Course it is. She needs to see them both. That's very kind of her. You two okay?"

"I think so. We had mad sex. Seems to calm her down."

"Eh?"

"Oh, Son's a strange one. You know how hysterical she can be. Remember the cat? When she gets like that, the only way I can calm her down, is with sex. It's like a release to her. It's like taking a pressure cooker of the heat. She was so wound up this time, I had to use the handcuffs."

"Handcuffs?!?"

"Yeah, she loves that, drives her insane, I told you. We've, well she that is, have four pink fluffy handcuffs and I__"

"Ok Rick too much information."

"No, seriously try it. They love it."

"Rick, stop! The last thing Yvonne would enjoy is THAT!"

"You don't know until you try."

"Rick! Stop."

"What? She bought them, not me."

"Rick! Enough! I like Son and I don't need to know personal stuff like that. Thank you."
Rick looked a bit wounded.

"Come on," I said, "it's all okay, we should get over to see Gary and see what's occurring."

"Okay thanks, I'll get these."

Rick paid, and we left Aroma. The fresh air felt good. It was a crisp autumn day, and everything felt normal again. The last 24 hours were a nightmare that I thought I'd never wake up from, but I had, and I felt massively relieved. The coffees had kicked in and I widened my stride.

Yvonne let Sonja in.

"Hi!" she said, and they both hugged in the hall. "Where is he?"

"Hi Son. He's in his bed. We can go up if you want."

"You okay?" Sonja asked Yvonne, I'm so sorry. Rick's been such an idiot. I clobbered him when he got home."

"I bet you did." Yvonne said, in exasperation.

"God, it must've been awful for you. What happened? Rick said Ed came into the bedroom and saw it all."

"He did, and panicked, and ran. Ran right past me and into the bus. So glad he never went under it."

"Yvonne," Sonja started to get hysterical.

"Shhh," Yvonne said, pointing to the ceiling.

"It's okay, it really is. It's going to be fine. You might get a shock when you see him."

"What? No… Poor…"

"Son, get a grip, he's okay, just a bit bruised but that will go and he's in plaster….."

"Oh my God, the poor lad."

"Come on, let's go say hello. He'd liked to see you. He actually thought it was funny, what Rick did."

"Really? He's okay with it?"

"Yes, you know how they are really fond of each other, I don't think that's been damaged."

"Thank Christ for that."

"Come on." Yvonne reassured Sonja, and took her by the arm towards the stairs.

"Ed. Look who's come to see you."

"Hi Son. How are you? Like my new tracksuit?"

"Oh Ed!" Sonja started.

Yvonne nudged her hard with her arm.

"You ok? Oh my little darling. Give me a kiss," and she moved towards him.

Ed screwed up his nose, said "Ow," and let Sonja kiss him on his good cheek.

"Careful." Called out Yvonne.

Ed got his kiss and Son sat on the bed.

"Oh look at you." Son said, stroking his hair.

"I am okay Son, really l am. Mum said if I'm still hungry that's a good sign!"

Even in his state of tumultuous stress, Ed still made people smile. I was so proud of the way he handled all of this. Showing his true character. His first real knock in his young life and probably not his last, but if this is how he's going to cope with things, he's going to be fine I thought. The three sat talking for a while. Ed regaling his adventure, telling Son all about the hospital tellies and so on, then Yvonne noticed he was getting tired and suggested to Son they leave him for now.

"Come back with Ricky." Ed said as they were leaving.

"I will," Son said, "still speaking to him?"

"Yeah of course. Silly Rick doing something like that."

Ed fell asleep. Yvonne and Son had tea and talked the whole thing through again.

"Can I do anything?" Son would ask.

"No, I've taken some compassionate leave for a couple of weeks. They've been very understanding about the whole thing. They said to come back when I'm ready."

"Oh no, does that mean you won't get paid? I can come around and sit with him if you want."

"No, it's ok Son. Thank you that's very kind. I'll get sick pay it'll be fine."

"That's good," Son said, "but just ask, won't you?"

"Yes I will, thanks."

Gary was on the phone as I knocked and entered the office.

"Sorry." I whispered

Gary beckoned us in, and gestured us to sit down, pointing at the coffee machine, no, I indicated, with my arm out, palm up, then I did a thumbs up, to say thanks. Gary was listening intently,

"Yeah…. sure…… ok. That sounds good… Well actually, they've just arrived… Yeah… I will…" Then a snigger and a rolling of his eyes… "Yeah, well you can tell him that." He said to the voice on the phone, nodding at Rick. Rick shuffled uncomfortably and crossed his legs.

"Ok, gotta go. See you on Friday, at Hemel."
He looked at me for confirmation. I nodded and gave a thumbs up.

"Yeah Friday it is. I'll tell the boys. I'm sure they'll be pleased."
Rick uncrossed his legs.

"Ok ciao." Gary hung up the call.

He glared at Rick for what seemed a long time, but was probably only a few seconds.

"You fucking dick!" He directed at Rick.
Rick crossed his legs again.

"What were you thinking of? I've spent all morning trying to placate Rank. They've all been on the phone. Ted wanted to know what the hell went on. The top knobs in Rank wanted to know what was going on. I've been instructed by Craig to give you the bollocking of your life, and to assure him nothing like that happens again. What the fuck, Rick?"

Rick had his head down then apologised and assured Gary it wouldn't happen again. There was a long silence. Gary was red with rage.

"You ok?" He asked me.

"Yeah, considering."

"What?"

"I don't think you've heard."

"What?"

Rick groaned in his seat and crossed his legs twice.

"What!" Demanded an exasperated Gary.

"After the show Rick came back with a couple of girls and put that plastic doll in bed with me for a laugh. I was out for the count and didn't know. Sunday morning, Yvonne and Ed turned up to surprise me, on my birthday."

"Oh no, and they saw it and you've got some explaining to do?"

"Worse than that."

Rick was squirming in his chair, head in his hands. Gary picked up on this and looked at me for an answer. He shrugged his shoulders as if to say 'well'?

"Er…?" I started.

"Oh shit." Came from a muffled Rick, still head in hands. Gary was becoming really agitated.

"Ok, it wasn't really Rick's fault." I started.

"Ed and Yvonne came into the room. The door had been left open. They'd brought my birthday breakfast that I have every year, it's a tradition. We do the same thing for each other. Ed bolted out of the room, out of the hotel, and was hit by a bus. He's__"

"What?" Gary exploded. Glaring at Rick. Rick was hoping the ground would swallow him up.

"He's ok. Broken arm, broken ribs. Going to be fine."

"Broken bones and he's going to be fine?"

"Gary, it's ok. Rick isn't really to blame. I didn't know they were coming."

Gary leapt out of his chair and launched a tirade of abuse at Rick. Gary never liked him, or trusted him. Rick made him nervous. He thought Rick was a waste of space.

"You fucking stupid cunt. When will you ever learn? You've got to reign this in, you idiot, or one day.... one day.... You'll kill someone. Jesus Christ. What is in that fucking sick head of yours? Hey? Hey?"

"Chris knows I'm sorry. I never meant anything like that to happen. Not to Ed, not to anyone. Chris knows I love Ed__"

"Gary, it's ok." I said trying to calm him down.

"Fuck me. You've got some friend there." He said to Rick, pointing at me.

"I'd never forgive you for doing that to one of mine."

"It's ok, really." I said. "Ed thinks it was just a joke, and his spirit is solid."

"Yvonne?" Gary asked.

"We are good. It's all sorted. Everything is fine. We are just waiting for Ed to mend, yes it could have been much, much, worse, but it isn't. So, let's go ahead now and put this behind us."

"Can I send some flowers for Yvonne? And what can I get Ed?" Gary asked.

"Yes, that would be much appreciated thank you. Ed would love anything. He's only got the use of one arm at the moment, but maybe a fire engine jigsaw or something like that, and Yvonne can do it with him."

"Ok, leave it with me. Fucking hell, I can't believe this."

He glared at Rick. Rick was shrinking into his seat.

"Rick" I said.

Rick looked up.

"It's fine buddy ok? We have to move on, it wasn't your fault, no one is blaming you."

"Son is." Rick replied and shrunk back even more into his seat.

"Alright," I tried to snap us all out of it, "what's happening? What do we have to be pleased about?"

Gary was sitting down now.

"Well apart from the bollockings I have to dish out__"

"Yeah, we've done that. Rick is staying, or we both walk."

Rick looked up at me, partly in disbelief, partly grateful, I don't think anyone has ever stuck up for him before. I'd rather move on with Rick than work for Rank without him.

"Hang on." Gary said with an arm up.

"No." I was seeing red now. "Rick stays and we move on or we both go."

"I haven't said he's getting fired." Gary growled.

"No, because you can't fire either of us. It's both of us, or fuck all for Rank".

"Chris__"

"I'm sorry Gary, I've had a shite weekend. Let's get going on moving this forward. Tell us what Rank said about the weekend, cos believe me, I saw the numbers. The takings must be eye watering. Not because of me, but him." I pointed at Rick. "He is the genius one here, what he did was amazing, you were there, the crowd loved it. Rank must have banked thousands. So, stick your bollockings up Rank's arse and let's go forward. WHAT, do we have to be pleased about? Because believe me, any good news would be welcomed right now."

Rick turned to me. Sheer shock on his face, and a love I'd seen in his eyes before, it was mainly when things came together on stage, mainly when he was playing in a seedy piano dive somewhere, but this look was for me. I loved the guy, he could be a complete arse sometimes, but I've never heard anyone, get a piano to sound like the way he could make it sound. I loved the bonding we had.

"Thanks mate." He mumbled.

Gary was now not so lobster red. He sat back down and twiddled his fingers on his desk, mimicking piano playing. The intercom burst the silence, and the atmosphere.

"Mr. Sproule on line one."

"I'M OUT!" Growled Gary.

The intercom clicked off loudly.

"Want coffee?" He gestured to the machine.

"No thanks, I'm all coffeed out." I said.

Rick got up and started to get one, more for something to do, than for needing another coffee.

"Alright." Gary blew out a loud, long sigh.

"Shit." He rubbed his eyes, and scrubbed his hair and began, "Well, ok. Rank were furious with Rick. They asked me to reign him in, or he can go. I did fight his cause, saying I would have words and get him to control himself, and that you, Chris, knew him better than anyone else, and I've trusted you to 'manage', Rick."

He made those quotation marks with his fingers.

"I knew Rick wouldn't listen to Rank almighty, but you could handle him, and that was good enough for me."

"Him?" Retorted Rick.

"Shut the fuck up, Rick." l said and gave him one of my 'behave yourself' looks.

Rick sat down.

"Ok, we sorted that out. Now; what's to please us?"

"Rank want to do a massive promo at the Dorchester hotel in Park Lane. They are inviting entertainment companies from all over Europe. They want to franchise the concept. Roll it out internationally."

"And they want us to do a show?"

Gary shuffled uncomfortably.

"Well they want you to do it and pick who you like to do it with you."

"Well I pick Rick." I said. "There is no one else out there that can get anywhere near him."

"But they're nervous__"

"It's Rick," I said, "or you find another two."

"The thing is__"

"Rick will behave. I guarantee that, and Rick will blow them all away. They won't forget what they will see, and Ray and Paul are the best you can get. We can do this, it will be great, you know that. Trust me on this one Gary." Gary agreed, reluctantly.

"So, when is this happening?" I asked.

"Early December. Rank want all the VIPs to see London's Christmas lights. They think it will help. Well, they are pretty impressive."

"Ok, anything we need to do? Hope it's not dressing up in Santa outfits." I said.

"Oh fuck. No…" said Rick

"Rick! Shut it!"

Rick let out a loud sigh and looked at the ceiling.

Gary gave me a 'see' glance.

"It's ok." I reassured him.

"Ok, we'll re-group next month for that one. Now the figures for the weekend. They're impressive. Beat Hemel's best."

"And that was us" said Rick.

"Knock it off." I said.

Gary continued, "The weekend gross was over £5,000 at the door and approximately £25,000 in sales. But they gave away lots of freebies, so the nett might not be so clever."

"What! That's bonkers money," I said, "and they'll be getting that plus for a while, without freebies. What about merchandising? That should offset the 'freebies'."

"Figures not in yet. But I bet they are great."

"Wow! Good. I need to get home to see how Ed is. We'll be okay for Hemel this weekend and maybe you could give us Hemel for a few more weekends. I don't fancy Brighton for a while yet, and it'll be good to get home every night."

"Yeah sure." Gary said.

"Ok with you Rick?" I asked.

"Yeah sure. I love Hemel, it rocks."

We shook hands and left Gary to do his managing. I was interested why Mr. Sproule, an old agent of mine, was ringing Gary. He either had players to introduce to Gary, or new venues to fill. I hoped it was new venues because he mainly operated in Amsterdam and I loved it there. Only weekend stuff, so do-able, and solo work…….Hmmmm.

"Wanna come back and see Ed? Son is probably still there. You can pick her up at the same time. Do me a favour, don't stay too long, I need a bit of time with Yvonne."

"Sure thing. Thanks. Hope he's still talking to me!"

"Oh, he thinks you're a real gas."

Yvonne and Sonja were having a cup of something at the kitchen table, and a good natter, by the sounds of it.

"Hi you two!" I announced ourselves to them.

"Hi." they both replied.

Then another less enthusiastic "Hi" to Rick, as he appeared behind me.

"Jesus Rick, you have no idea how serious this is. You don't know what you've put us through. What were you thinking?" Yvonne was truly angry with him. Justifiably so, I thought.

"Sorry Yvonne, sorry. I never meant any of that to happen, especially to Ed. I love him to bits. I didn't know you were both coming down. Jesus, I didn't. I just thought it would be a gas and I just wanted to play a joke on Chris. Really that's all it was. I'm so sorry it went so wrong."

Yvonne gave Rick a stare. She was good at those.

"Come on let's go see Ed." I indicated to Rick.

We went up the stairs two at a time and found Ed sitting up in anticipation. He'd heard us downstairs obviously.

"Hi." he blurted out.

"Hi matey." I said, giving him a kiss on the forehead.

"Hi buddy." Rick sat on the bed. "Blimey look at you! I'm so sorry Ed. This is all my fault."

"Nah, it's not." Ed said bravely. "You were just goofing around, I know, and sticking that thing in Dad's bed; Ha Ha! Bet that would have frightened him first thing in the morning!"

"So sorry bud. I mean it." Rick said, apologetically We spent a bit of gentle time with Ed. No jokes, no making him laugh. Then I gave Rick the nod.

"Time to go." l said to him.

"Aw!" Ed protested.

"Come on, have a kip." I said tucking him in.

"Can you ask Mum to bring some squash up please?"

"Sure, I can manage that." I said.

Downstairs, Son was putting her coat on.

"I'll just run up to say goodbye to Ed." she said.

"Thanks for dropping by Rick. Appreciate it."

"That's ok Yvonne, least I can do. If you need anything__"

"Thanks, we'll be fine. Call you if we do."

"Ok. Great."

Son appeared, and we hugged, then they left. Time on our own. God, we need it.

I got Ed some squash. Yvonne put the kettle on.

"We need to talk." She said.

Chapter 15

I guessed what was coming, and I was right.

"Rick is out of control. He nearly killed our son."

"Yvonne, he didn't. He never__"

"Let me finish." Yvonne said, with an outstretched arm, palm up to me.

"Go on. Sorry."

"I know you love him in a guy, matey, type way. I know how close you two are. I know you think he's a great musician, a showman, I even guess you want to be like that, but you're too 'straight', grounded, or whatever you want to call it. I love you for being you, I'd never entertain Rick, or you as Rick, for anything. Why Son puts up with it, I don't know."

"Rick is__"

"Let me finish. Then you can have your say, and I won't interrupt."

"Ok."

"I 'get' it, I 'get' you two. You're brilliant together. The times I've seen you both playing together have been amazing. Rick is one note short of imploding, but he always manages to keep it together."

"You DO understand!" I interrupted.

"Chris! But YOU, are the anchor, the perfectionist. The planner. You make this a success, and with or without Rick, you would have done it, and I'm so proud of you. I know Rick didn't really nearly kill Ed but…" Yvonne blew out a loud, long sigh, and sat back in the kitchen chair. She was exasperated. She'd been through such a lot, and even saw Ed bounce off that bus. God that must have been devastating. I was beside myself when I came out and saw him lifeless in the road. My whole world collapsed around me, or so very nearly did. I couldn't be angry with Rick. I saw the look on his face when he came out of the hotel. He was mortified too, and I knew he would blame himself. He felt responsible for what happened, and in a way, he was, in a way, he wasn't. He had no idea they were coming down, and if they hadn't, Ed would have been be ok, and I would have put it down to one of Rick's gags and laughed it off. I would have even told Ed and Yvonne about it, and they would have rolled their eyes and shook their heads. They probably would've laughed too, I guess.

"Yvonne, I'm so sorry you had to see that. Thank God you were there to attend to him, anyone else might have tried to pick him up, or get him off the road. I was so proud of you too. Taking over like you did. You have so much knowledge and you are so calm and professional. You are amazing. You saved his life."

"Oh, Chris It was just me doing my job."

"Yes, but in those circumstances? Wow! You were amazing. What can I do about Rick? I've talked to him about his behaviour, especially towards Son, who idolizes him, don't know why, I agree with you. Maybe she sees the good part in Rick. I know somewhere in there he has a big heart, and all this rock image or whatever you want to call it is a front, maybe an act, but Rick is the best piano player by miles that I've ever met, and the crowd love him. He even makes my job easier."

"Well can't you reign him in even more? Get him to take life more seriously."

"I think he will after what has happened. It's really shocked him to the bone. I'll go out for a drink with him, see how he is, try talking a bit of sense into him, but Yvonne, you know Rick doesn't do 'sense'."

"It's not what Rick does or doesn't do. He is a loose cannon and I'm nervous of what he'll do next."

"Nothing that will harm Ed, I'm sure."

"Yeah, you're right, but please have a word. He listens to you, and make it plain, we are not at all happy with him, this or anything else, just get the message over to him to behave a bit. I know Rick doesn't do 'behave' either, but…"

"Ok, leave it to me."

"What do you want for dinner?"

"You." I said, and she playfully slapped my face. She got up and started preparing some vegetables.

"Ok if we just have soup and a roll?" She asked.

"Yeah, great. I love your soups."
"Don't feel like much. Do you?"
"No, not really."
"We have to eat something, and I can blitz some for Ed."
"Ok, sounds good to me."
"So, what happened in the office with Gary? Rick get a bollocking?"

It was strange hearing Yvonne use that word. She never swore, until Ed was in danger that is. I opened a bottle of red and poured out two large ones. I leaned against the worktop and admired Yvonne's expert, chef like chopping.

"Bollocking? Gary tried to fire him."
"Fire him? Crikey. He's in that much trouble? What happened?"
"Well Rank wanted him out, or sorted out, and told Gary in no uncertain terms to deal with him."
"What did Rick say to that?"
"Nothing, he had his head buried in his hands. I told Gary that wasn't going to happen__"
"Chris! YOU can't tell Gary anything, surely?"
"Well I did. I told Gary it's the two of us, or we both walk."
"Christ Chris, you need this job, you've worked so hard for it. Don't throw it away just because of Rick."
"I won't. But I'm not doing it without him. There is no one else out there I want to play with. We could take the concept on the road. I don't know, we could work

something out. I told Gary to leave Rick to me, and I guaranteed he will be ok, let's face it, he has been up to now. No one expected this."

"Did Gary know? About Ed, I mean."

"No, and when I told him I thought he was going to jump over his desk and chin Rick. He launched a shed load of abuse at him, and said he was very lucky to have me as a friend and to pull himself together and man up and so on."

"Jesus." Yvonne said, taking her frustration out on a leek.

We sat down while the soup was cooking. Delicious, delicate, smells, filled the kitchen. I sat opposite Yvonne and put my hands out across to her. She instinctively put hers out and we held hands and just looked at each other for a minute or two.

"I love you." She said. "I couldn't bear it if anything happened to you, or Ed again. I wish you would get a job teaching, but I know this is your life and I'm ok with it really. I know how happy you are and I'm happy for you."

"Thank you. That means a lot." I said squeezing her hands. She squeezed back, and we drank our wine and chatted about this and that, until Yvonne's instinctive timing meant the soup was ready.

"I'll whiz it if you can warm some rolls on the toaster." She said.

"Ok, I'm on it, can I have mine unwhizzed?"

"Of course. I'll only whiz Ed's. I like mine chunky too."

We took our soup upstairs, and sat with Ed. Everything felt normal, except I would wince when Ed flinched or twitched, in pain. It wasn't a pleasant sight but at least he was ok, thank God he was ok. We had a lovely chat about his new tracksuit, about the lovely nurses, and doctors that looked after Ed.

"Can't believe they did all this just for me!" He said. "Is that what you do at work Mum?"

"Yes darling. I do that every time I'm there, just like those lovely nurses that looked after you."

"You look after little boys too?" Asked Ed, tucking into his soup. Glad he was eating. Always a good sign Yvonne would say.

"Yep. Little tigers like you."

Ed visibly beamed.

"And old codgers like your Dad!"

"Ha! Ha! Ouch!" Ed spluttered.

"Oi!" I said, pulling a horrid face at Ed.

"Dad's not old Mum," he'd say, he's just getting on a bit."

"Watch it." I said to Ed, pointing my spoon at him.

"Love you Dad. You're the best Dad ever. All the other kids say how funny you are, and they love it when they come here. Love you too Mum, you're the best Mum ever. Everyone says you make the best food in the world."

"What, even better than McDonald's?"

"Yeah of course!"

"What do you get when you go round to their's?"

"Oh pizza, or beans on toast, we never get anything like this." Ed nodded towards his soup. "It's brilliant. Thanks Mum."

"Oh sweetheart. You're the best little boy ever."

"You certainly are." I said, taking his empty bowl away. "I'm so proud of you." Ed leaned in for his hug. We hugged for a while. I could feel his breathing. He felt content and I knew he was so happy with his life, and we were euphoric at the love and joy he had brought us.

"Come on." Said Yvonne. "Let's get you to the loo and ready for bed."

"Can I keep my tracksuit on?"

"I think your peejays would be better. You'll get too hot in that." pointing at the tracksuit.

"Oh Mum, please!"

"Ed, come on let's get you sorted."

"I'll sort these out." I said with the dishes in my hand, and I'll come back up and tuck you in, chunky monkey."

"Ok Dad, don't forget!"

Yvonne gently maneuvered Ed to the bathroom and washed him while he sat on the loo. I heard the odd "OW!" and "Muuum….!" I cleaned up downstairs, and thought about how I was going to tackle Rick. I knew that he knew he'd overstepped the mark. But that's Rick. He loves to shock people or antagonize them. He loved winding them up just to see them squirm. He did it with me so often, and I was used to him now, but he still managed to press the odd button now and again. I still loved the guy though, just have to kick his arse right now.

Yvonne appeared and said to go up, Ed wouldn't be awake long. I ran up, and tucked him in. He was asleep before I left the room. We crashed out on the sofa. One of my favourite times together with Yvonne. I would sit one end, she would sit the other, facing me with her legs over mine. I would stroke her feet. She loved that, especially after a long day at work.

"You ok?" I asked her.

"Yeah. Always ok with you here."

"Love you."

"I know," she said, "love you too."

"I'll talk to Rick. Get him to think about his actions, and try to make him realise how they affect people, especially Son."

"Oh, I feel so sorry for her, but she loves Rick and I'm not sure we can do anything about that. At the end of the day it's her choice. What can WE do? I'll talk to her anyway. I'm sure she'll be around a lot offering support, and that's very sweet of her, I'll handle Son, and you handle Rick. Ok?"

We chatted a bit more, finished the wine, and headed up to bed. We fell fast asleep, arms and legs wrapped around each other.

Chapter 16

"Hi Rick. What you up to?"
It was Tuesday. I thought I had better square things with Rick before Friday's gig at Hemel.
"Hi man. You ok? Ed, and Yvonne?"
"Yeah we're good, Ed's comfy, and Yvonne is doing a great job."
"Oh good. They still speaking to me?"
"Yes of course, don't worry. What are you doing this week?"
"I'm doing a night in Roxy's tomorrow if you wanna come along and join in." Rick often played there, doing his 'alternative' set, which consisted of material totally opposite to our set. Such delights from the likes of Dr John, J.J. Cale, and Tom Waits, and anything Blues. I would occasionally turn up, and we'd do four hands on the piano. It certainly was very self-indulgent but worked brilliantly. The audience loved it. I loved it. At one, with my best mate. Rick lapping it up, and we occasionally gave each other appreciative nods, as something suddenly gelled and we hit a 'high'.

Nothing else could beat that feeling. Nothing.

"Yeah that sounds like a plan. See you there about nine?"

"Great. Everything ok?"

"Yeah just wanna hang, that's all. Look forward to it."

"Ok, see you tomorrow. Take care and say 'Hi' to them both. Son's saying 'Hi' too."

"Hi back. See you mate."

I hung up and scratched my head. How do I run this by Rick, without upsetting him? I'm sure it will just come out when I see him.

"Sproule was on the phone to Gary when we were in the office". I said to Yvonne who had just appeared after sorting Ed out.

"Yeah?"

"I think I might wander down there, maybe Gary has some info on work. Might be nice to have a break from Rick."

"Wow. You have been thinking about what we talked about."

"Of course I have. It may mean a couple of nights away, if it's Amsterdam."

"Go for it. I'll miss you but you may be right about some time out from Rick. What will Rick do when you're away, and would that be okay with Gary?"

"Oh yeah. He'd love it if Rick stayed away for a gig or two. Oh, and by the way I've just got off the phone with Rick and said I'd meet him in Roxy's for a chat tomorrow. Is that ok with you."

"Of course it is. I know you like it there, and I'm not going anywhere." She said, nodding up to the ceiling. I smiled and said,

"You should get some free time too. Go out whenever you feel like it. I can take care of Ed. Don't want you getting cabin fever. How's your Mum? Go and have lunch or something or take a night off and go out with your mates."

"Thank you, sweetie, I will, but I'm ok, thanks for offering."

"Well he's no trouble, is he?" I nodded upstairs.

"A tough little thing." Yvonne said.

"He hasn't complained once."

"That's my boy." I said. "Yes, take time out whenever you want. We'll be ok."

Yvonne came close and kissed me. We held each other for a moment. Suddenly all was well in the world.

"Ok, let me ring Gary and I'll shoot off to see him. That alright with you? If you need to do something, it can wait."

"No. Go on, I'm curious too."

I called Gary and asked if we could meet for lunch and a chat. He agreed, I think he wanted to talk to me on my own anyway. I asked Yvonne if she needed anything while I was out, she didn't, and wished me luck.

"Hiya, come in and take a seat I'll only be a few minutes." Gary gestured to the chair.

"Coffee? Help yourself."

"Thanks, I'll wait. Where do you fancy lunch? Got enough time to go out?"

"Yeah sure. Not much happening today and I've got something to run by you that might interest you."

Sounds hopeful I thought. Gary's desk was a joke. Complete organized mayhem, I thought. Papers everywhere. Ring binders piled high, some open, the contents spilling out. Just about every music publication imaginable scattered over the chairs, and on the floor. Piles of CDs, probably from budding pianists, stage acts, stand ups, all wanting his attention. Gary finished scribbling on his pad, clicked the intercom and said,

"Hi Jen. I'm off out for an hour. Anything there for me?"

"No, you're good to go. Have fun. Don't forget Abby's birthday Sunday."

"Oh yeah! Cheers. Thanks for that Hun."

"No probs," and the intercom clicked off.

"You need reminding of your wife's birthday!" I asked.

"No, already fixed something, but she's great." He said nodding at the intercom. "Doesn't miss a thing. Where shall we go?

"I don't mind, the Firkin pub is just over the road and the sarnies are always good."

"Great. Let's go."

The Firkin chain of pubs, started by a Mr. David Bruce in the 80s, were champions of what a typical English pub should be, but with attitude. No gaming machines, no carpet, some sawdust for effect, a brewery in the cellar brewing notable ales such as "Dogbolter", a mistake which turned out to be a delicious, malty, rich beer, and a piano. I've had so many bonkers nights in quite a few of them. Far too many to list here, maybe that's another book for another time. Just one extra special moment happened in the Frog and Firkin, West London. I took my parents there when they visited me from the north-east. The Frog was going mental, as usual. My Dad was standing on the table, conducting the singing, when in came the Reading chapter of Hell's Angels. I wasn't too worried, but felt that my parents might be. The night went brilliantly and after I had finished playing, I couldn't find my Dad.

"He's outside". Mum said, looking a tad worried.
I went out to find him astride the meanest Harley, trying to kickstart it! With several bikers encouraging him!

"It's ok," one said to me, "I've got the keys!"
He held them up to show me. "Your Dad's a bloody hero mate," he said, "used to ride BSA's in Czechoslovakia in the war. I said he could take mine for a spin if he could start it!"

Brilliant times, brilliant memories.

"What you having?" Gary asked. "Don't worry it's on expenses."

"Pint of Dog and a beef bap please."

They only did two kinds of bap, Beef and onion or cheese and onion, designed to soak up the beer.

We took our fayre and found a quiet spot by the window. I loved pubs during the daytime. They were quiet, as if they were resting. A 'downtime' for pubs, I thought, after an evening of noise, mayhem, and drunks, drinking staggering amounts of alcohol.

"Oh, that's good, really good." Gary said, smacking his lips and diving into his bap.

"Had some great times in here." I said. "Some hairy ones too, but always made it out alive!"

"Yeah first time I ever saw you was in the Goose and Firkin in the Elephant, (and Castle). I couldn't work out where the music was coming from, as I couldn't see you! Must've been pretty scary!"

"It was some nights, but never really had too much trouble. They were all too drunk, I think!"

"Anyway", started Gary, still with his mouthful. "How's Ed? Yvonne taking good care of him?"

"Yeah, he's great, a tough little bugger, and Yvonne is doing a great job. Lucky to have her, he'll be up on his feet in no time, his spirit amazes me. He always has a smile. He's an inspiration."

"Rick?"

"Yeah I've talked to him and I'm meeting him tomorrow for more. He's playing in Roxy's. Why don't you drop by, and see the other side of him? He's quite brilliant."

"Can't believe your loyalty sometimes. I'd have you as a mate in a heartbeat."

"We are mates, aren't we?"

"Yeah, suppose so." Gary smiled, and continued, "Well it's kind of last chance saloon now with Rick, as regards to Rank. You must make him aware that anything else like this and he's out. I'm trusting you to reign him in and control him. I've put my neck on the line to keep him on board. I just reminded Rank of the numbers and they eased off a bit."

"Ok, cheers for that. I'll keep him on track. I'm sure he'll behave; he loves this job."

"Good. I've got something you might want to consider, and it will give Rick some time out from Rank also. Sproule has been in touch wanting some guys for Amsterdam and Scheveningen in Holland. I didn't even think of you two at first but then I thought why not? Rick and Rank could have their space. It's only a few weekends and I know you like it there."

"Love it. Can I do Amsterdam. Maxime's?"

"Yep, that's the one."

"I'll never forget the first time you rang me about that job, and said I had to pick up the keys for the apartment, from the sex shop next door! Sounds interesting I thought, and it was! What a dive. The black hole of Calcutta I called it. Loads of rich businessmen with their escorts. The tips were mind blowing! Klaus still there?"

"Yep. Still moaning about expenses and taxes, it's just to get my price down, but I'm not having any of it, he's rolling in it. I'll run a few dates by you and see what you want. Start looking at flights, if you like, and we can pick a cheap time."

"Ok, great, thanks. I'll tell Rick, he's going to Sheveningen, he'll be up for that."

"Good. Now there's a big push coming up at the Dorchester just before Christmas."

"Oh yeah. What's that all about?"

Gary explained how Rank wanted to franchise the Duelling Pianos concept. Roll it out to other venues and other countries across Europe. The show was to be a one nighter, a whole concept of Jumpin' Jaks. That meant the routines (please change the name of Hillbillies on Fire, I would protest to Gary), the lookalikes, (the good ones were great, a bad Freddie was disastrous,) and of course the Duelling Pianos. We were to do a one hour set at the end of the night, and hopefully leave them impressed and want to sign the concept up.

"Sounds good." I said, very keen to show Gary I was up for it. With Rick of course.

"If Rick behaves, they'll let him do it, but please don't blow this one, it's huge."

"I know, don't worry. Rick will be fine. I think he's still in shock over what's happened."

"Oh, and you get a room each in the hotel. They've taken every available room and want to please everyone on this one. Keep it quiet though, it's only for artists. The staff might get upset if they smell favouritism."

"Wow! Great, sounds fab."

We finished our beer and sandwiches. Gary wanted to get back to the office, and I didn't fancy drinking any more, not really a lunchtime drinker, except Sundays, when you could go home, to a roast and then sleep it off. I headed home, I'd tell Rick the news tomorrow, at Roxy's. He'll probably like the space, and he'll love the gigs. Sheveningen, on the west coast of Holland, was a lively place. They often did Duelling Pianos there, and the solo work was good.

I bought some spray roses for Yvonne and a couple of bottles of Shiraz for us both and found a Lego fire engine I could do with Ed, and his good arm later.

Curry smells greeted me at the door, with the biggest smile, and hug I could wish for, from Yvonne.

"Wow! Hi! You ok?"

"Yes, just missed you that's all." She said, giving me a long warm hug.

"For you." I said holding out the flowers.

"Wooh, lovely! She said.

"For us!" Holding up the wine.

"Hmmm, let's start now."

"And this is for Ed. Maybe we can do it together."

"Oh, he'll love that. You could do it under his instruction, he loves showing you how."

"Great smell by the way."

I ran up to see Ed. He was dozing but livened up when I came in with a toy shop bag.

"Hi Dad! What's that?"

"Got this for you. Thought you could help me make it."

"Aw great yeah I'll show you."

"Come on then, shouldn't take long. Dinner is nearly ready, judging by the smell. You had a good day?"

"Yeah, Mum's been up and down. Maybe I can come down onto the sofa tomorrow."

"Don't see why not, if it's ok with Mum."

We made the fire engine in twenty minutes. Ed loved it. Yvonne brought dinner up, and we ate it together. We got Ed settled in for the night, and retired to the sofa, Yvonne with her feet up over my legs.

"So, tell me about your day." She asked.

Chapter 17

The usual feet sticking to the floor told me I was well and truly inside Roxy's. It used to be thick pile carpet, but was now a flattened solid matt of dried beer, champagne, puke, and probably some blood somewhere, and the smell to go with it. The facade outside, certainly belied what was inside. Once a luxurious den of debauchery, opulence, secret goings on under the tables, with hostesses and sex starved men desperate for any action, even paying £100 plus for cheap champagne. To get a late licence, they had to have live music, that enabled them to stay open until 2am. The obvious choice was a pianist. Laid-back, and cost effective. Over the years Roxy's had built up a name for themselves as a cosy place to hang out. Tasty Tapas were served, along with any drink you fancied, mainly cocktails. They only served bottled beer, so no cellar here, just a quick turnaround of stock, they bought in, sold for a profit, and struggled to keep the place open, but open it was, and long may it last. It wasn't really my scene, but Rick loved it. They loved him. He played all the sophisticated jazz, and smoochy cocktail bar numbers, but gave them an attitude. There was a certain electricity in the room when Rick was entertaining. Other guys and girls sometimes just turned up, played, got paid, and went home, looking bored most of the time. But Rick didn't do 'bored'. Rick was playing 'Closing Time', a Tom Waits classic, and I could tell immediately who he was singing it to. His eyes were drilled into a smart looking businesswoman, sitting alone two tables away and totally engrossed in Rick. A bottle of white was in a cooler on her table, and she seemed very comfortable with Rick's attention. I felt like slapping him as I walked past him.

"Oi! Behave!" I said, as he hadn't even noticed me. Not a hesitation, "Hi" back, or anything, Rick was totally engrossed in his work and in winning the attention of someone that night. I ordered a San Miguel and sat at the bar. Rick was truly on form. Loving his art. Working the room, only right now he was working the captivating lady, and knowing Rick, getting horny, which seemed to make him play better. He gave me a subtle nod and carried on singing directly to that beautiful lady on table six. Will you ever behave? I thought.

Rick finished the number to rapturous applause, and shouts for more. He announced his break, went over and said something into the lady's ear, and came over to me, pulling a bar stool a little closer.

"Hey man, you made it! Great to see you!"

The Barman handed him a drink. It looked like Coke, but I could smell the JD.

"Thanks man." Rick cheered, with his glass, his new friend, a few tables away. She smiled and shuffled in her seat, sipping her wine.

"Come on mate? Seriously? Can't you leave it alone ever?"

"What for?" He protested.

"Son." I said.

"Christ Chris, how many times have I told you, we are together, but she is free to do what she wants and so am I."

"But don't you think it's a bit unfair? She adores you and you don't seem to give a shit."

"I do. I do really. I'm there for her in any crisis. She knows that. I have told her I love her, but don't want to be tied down……"

"You're using her!"

"No, she's agreed to stay with me, said she needs me and doesn't mind what I get up to as long as I go back to her. Don't do this now, it's my business, thank you, and it's great to see you. Wanna do one together?"

"Yeah, of course."

"What about Leon Russell's Masquerade?"

"Yeah sure, you start it and I'll come up and join you."

"Great!"

We sat and chatted for a while. Rick was enthusiastic about his playing and was looking forward to Holland.

"Bet you picked Maxime's," he complained.

"Of course! I love it there, and I haven't seen Klaus for ages. It'll be good to get back, and the sea air will do you good, where you're going." I could not quite contain a snigger.

"Fuck off." Rick snarled, but I knew he would enjoy it.

"Look, we need a break from Rank. You, or we are hanging on by the skin of our teeth."

"Yeah, thanks for sticking by me, really appreciate that. Don't know what I'd be doing now, if I hadn't have met you. Cheers."

"I do. Cheers pal." I said, clinking our glasses.

"Yeah, I don't wanna go there, but seriously, you saved me. Cheers again."

"Go kill 'em," I said, "start Masquerade and I'll come and join you."

"Okay. See you in a bit."

"Careful with the lovely lady." I warned him.

Rick strutted past the beautiful lady, winked and gave an extra 'swagger', as he passed her. The crowd clapped and shouted out requests. Rick took his place at the piano, and very gently started playing Booker T and the MG's, Green Onions. No slamming his hand down hard here. Very subtle. Very tasty I thought. That's my Rick.

The crowd started clapping on the wrong beat, which I knew annoyed Rick immensely. He gave them a smile and carried on, resisting the urge to speed up as the crowd clapped more enthusiastically, and therefore tended to get faster. He kept it rock solid, building up the intensity, going off into a mind-blowing solo after solo and then suddenly dropping the volume and bringing it right down to hardly audible, but still there, still marching on. Such dynamics. Rick was a natural, a master of his trade, and loving every minute. A rather more subtle splat of a chord, and finished bang on time with a knowing nod to the crowd and of course a wink to you know who. She clapped over enthusiastically, and almost stood up. J.J. Cale's 'After Midnight' came next. So laid-back, so cool and with such a velvet vocal. Rick was in control, and loving it. A subtle nod to me on the end chord, signalled Masquerade was next up. I ordered another San Miguel and the bartender nodded an 'it's ok, you don't have to pay' nod, and I made my way over to Rick, who was into the first verse of Russell's classic. No vocal, just delicious licks, caresses, and crushed trills, where you play the note next to the correct one, and then slide onto the correct note.

I think it's called jazz.

I sat next to Rick, on his right side. He would slip back into rhythm piano and I would take the lead, or solo part. I tried so hard to underplay it, to be as cool as Rick, but he was hard to match. Eventually we found our rhythm and gelled into a symphony of four handed piano. When it works, it is truly orgasmic. We tapped our feet and swayed in unison.

Beautiful.

We finished Masquerade and Rick started 'Call me the Breeze' A J.J. Cale masterpiece, and the crowd settled down to jiving in their seats. The owner came and put two drinks on the piano and patted us both on our backs. He's happy, I thought, and so was I.
I left Rick to finish the set.

After winding up the crowd he left them for another break. We had to take breaks as this is when the crowd get to the bar and effectively 'pay us'. Rick took his stool next to mine, ignoring beautiful lady. I talked to him more about being responsible, and respectful to Rank (and Sonja) much to his disapproval but I think he was listening. We bear hugged, and I left him to finish his night. The barman thanked me, and invited me to come and do my own thing one night, I declined, saying Rick was his man, but I was delighted to come and join in.

"Any time, and don't leave it too long." He enthused.
Rick sat at the piano to a now rowdy crowd and gave me a knowing 'See you mate' nod and went into a melancholy 'Whole Lotta Shakin'. It worked quite well.

I walked home. It was a freezing cold crisp night, and I breathed in the refreshing air.
It was good to be alive.
Ed was snuffling.
Yvonne was sound asleep.
I sneaked in next to her and we spooned back to sleep.

Chapter 18

"Dad! Dad!" I heard Ed shouting, as I woke from a dead sleep. Not too worse for wear though, after my night out with Rick. I scrambled out of bed and into Ed's room.

"Yes buddy?" I asked Ed, who was trying to scratch his plastered arm.

"It's itchy Dad." He said, frantically trying to cure it by scratching the plaster. Distraction I thought. Yvonne was great at diffusing situations caused by bumps, and scrapes and minor upsets, by distracting Ed, so he forgot what had upset him in the first place.

"Want a bacon sandwich for brekkie?" I asked him.

"Yeah! Sounds good." He replied enthusiastically.

"Ok, need the loo first?" I asked him.

"Please."

I got Ed sorted and comfortable. He had forgotten his itchy arm already.

"Tea love?" I stuck my head back into our bedroom.

"Yeah. That would be great. Thanks." Yvonne stretched out and gave me one of her beautiful smiles. I made bacon sandwiches, and a large pot of tea, and then orange juice for Ed. I found Yvonne already sitting on Ed's bed. We had breakfast together and chatted about this and that.

"You out tonight?" Yvonne asked.

"Yeah, just up the road." which meant Hemel.

"Great. You'll be home later then."

"Yep, two minutes after closing." I joked.

"No!" drive carefully, rather you were back late, and not racing home."

"Ok you two, I'm off to see what's occurring. Have a good day and I'll see you before work tonight. Take care."

"See you Dad."

"See you darling." With a kiss from them both.

I rang Rick and suggested we meet up with the boys and told them what was happening. If we were going to Amsterdam for a weekend or three, they might want to find some dep work or just chill. Also needed to fill them in with the Dorchester hotel, and what may be required for that. We met at Aroma and enjoyed two perfect flat whites. I arranged we got there before the other two, just to chill and chat.

"Great to see you last night." Rick said, doing a 'cheers' with his coffee.

"Yeah, likewise, always like our jazzy moments."

"Masquerade went down well. Steve (the manager) wants me to persuade you to do your own gig down there. Why don't you? You love it as much as I do, and the crowd dig it when you sit in. I look forward to you turning up, too."

"Yeah, like last night? How did you get on with Ms. businesswoman? You hardly noticed me walk by you."

"Course I did! Just playing it cool. We chatted; think she may have been a hooker. Nothing really gelled, so I legged it home. Good job too."

"Huh? Why?"

"Son had handcuffed herself to the bed, about half an hour before I was due home. If I hadn't gone home, she would still be there now!" He added with a gleeful smile.

"Rick, how could she handcuff herself to the bed?"

"Don't know, but she did."

"Maybe she wasn't alone."

"Nah, she wouldn't do that. Handcuffs are a me and her thing only."

She loves it when she can't stop me doing all sorts of naughty things to her, and I tease her to the limit then follow through to release the frustration. She goes absolutely bananas."

"Alright. Too much info there, Rick."

"No, you should try it. They love it."

"Son might. Yvonne? Never. Anyway, we have our own way of reaching supernova heights."

"Supernova?"

"Yeah, when we, or should I say Yvonne, has a rather, er, hmmm, 'special' one."

"Orgasm?"

"Yeah. We called it a 'Supernova'"

"Ha! I like that! Well Son has intercontinental ballistic super rollover novas!! Ha ha!!"

"Rick, where do you get it from?"

"Aw man, she just loves being handcuffed, tied up, spontaneous is always good too. We can't get enough".

"Then why not stop all this playing around and make an honest woman out of her?"

"Nah! We'd get bored. I know it. Me being on the edge, if you like, excites her and we get off on a lot of 'dirty' things if you see what I mean."

"Ok, enough about that. It'll be good to see Ray and Paul again. It seems like an age since last week.

"Yep, looking forward to tonight. Just want to let rip…"

"Be careful!! Remember what Gary said, you've got to tow the line for a bit. Don't want to piss off Rank completely".

"Tow the line? Puh! I'll behave, don't worry."

Ray and Paul arrived, and we ordered more coffee. They were both very concerned about us, Ed especially, and I thanked them. They brought a large, expensive bunch of flowers for Yvonne.

"What the fuck Rick?" Said Paul.

"I know, I know, I didn't mean any of that to happen, you know that. Just thought it would be a blast that's all."

"Surprised they didn't fire you", added Ray. "they're all such a bunch of square fuckers."

"They tried," Said Rick, and then pointed to me, and added, "but this one stuck up for me. Talked them out of it. Said it was me, or no one. Thanks buddy, I'll always owe you for that".

"Don't worry it's ok. Right!" I said. "Moving on. We've been given a few weekends in Amsterdam, to let the dust settle, I guess you two can either find a dep job, or Rank says you can sit in with Ian and Reg. If nothing comes up, they'll pay you a cancellation fee. Better than nothing."

"So, get a dep job and claim your cancellation fee!" Chipped in Rick.

"Alright Rick," I said, seriously now please."

"Not too shabby." Said Ray. "I always wanted to do the open mike at The Stag. Guess I can now."

"Yeah, and I'll probably just chill." Added Paul.

"How much is a cancellation fee?" Asked Rick. After a long pause, "I might cancel one."

"You only get it if Rank cancel, you moron." said Ray, puffing out his cheeks.

"Listen!" I said trying to contain a snigger.

"Unbelievable Rick!" Ray added.

"I was only joking?"

Not sure if Rick was 'only joking' or realised he had put his foot in it, and tried to rescue himself.

"Anyway, talk to Gary, he will fill you in on it. Think it's a one-er a night. Not bad for sitting in a bar drinking and getting paid at the same time."

"Ok. Sounds fine with me. Ray?"

"Yeah, sure. Good luck in Amsters, especially you Rick, God help them!"

"I'm being sent to the seaside," protested Rick.

"Scheveningen".

I was surprised he could actually pronounce it correctly.

"Oh well, God help them, wherever that is," mused Ray.

"Ok, Hemel tonight, and next weekend. I really don't fancy Brighton for a while."

"Don't blame you mate" said Paul.

"........and then three weekends after that we are away. Now there is a big, a really big do, coming up in December. Rank want a big show doing at the Dorchester Hotel, Park Lane, with a view to franchising the Duelling Pianos concept across Europe. Some big names coming and hopefully we can show them what we are best at, and they will sign some contracts. This is literally worth millions for Rank, and they're pulling out all the stops. They want the full show, lookalikes, stand-ups, and those bloody routines. If the VIPs can get past that without passing out, we should be able to blow their socks off, and get them to buy it. I hope they all say they just want to buy the piano bar part!"

"More work for us abroad?" Asked Paul.

"Doubt it. Maybe the openings, who knows? More work for me and Rick, as we have to train up more pianists."

"What's the bet, they'll use backing tracks?" Ray sniped.

"Hmmm maybe. Save them a lot of money." I said.

"Yeah, but not the same. Jeez!" Ray puffed.

"Alright. See you two later at Hemel. Me and Rick will meet with Gary and get some more info. I think the Dorchester is the first week in December. They want the Christmas lights and all, to impress them, should be a blast."

"Not a penguin suit?" Asked Ray, in disbelief.

"Nah, normal, we're the Duelling Pianos, not puppets."

"Thank Christ for that!" Said Ray.

We finished our coffee and split. Rick and I headed over to Gary's office, and hung around outside, until Jen said we could go in.

"Ok, Rick, please be as chilled as you can. No confrontation eh?"

"Yeah. I've got it. Don't worry."

The intercom buzzed, Jen answered it, and said, "Yes ok." into the handset. "You can go right in now." She said, nodding at Gary's office door.

"Cheers Jen."

Rick nodded in approval, and followed me in.

"Hi guys. Take a seat. Coffee?"

Gary was upbeat and smiling, even to Rick.

"Thanks, but we're all coffeed out." I looked at Rick, who nodded, and we sat down, opposite Gary's hilarious desk.

"Do you actually know where anything is?" I asked, nodding at the mayhem on his desk.

"Of course I do! Organized chaos this is. A tidy desk isn't a busy desk. Thank God mine isn't tidy. Anyway, are you both okay? Ed and Yvonne good?"

"Yeah, they're fine thanks, and Yvonne says thanks for the flowers. Very kind of you."

"No probs, and you Rick. All ok?"

"Yeah, fine thanks Gary. We did a stint in Roxy's; you must come down sometime. It's really cool."

"Yeah, I've heard you mention that place before. Let me know next time and I'll make an effort. Good, well I talked with Rank, and they are ok with Rick continuing, as long as there is no repeat of the last debacle, and I think a couple of weekends away is not a bad idea. Just the two. So, after next weekend the two weekends after are booked in Holland. Get your flights and I'll give you the contracts before you go. I know it's short notice, and the flights may be more expensive, so I persuaded Rank to cough up £100 towards them. Hope that's ok?"

"Cool." Said Rick.

"On your return, we'll start the prep for The Dorchester. Rank are quite excited, and one top knob said he hoped Rick didn't reel it in too much."

"Oh God. I wish you hadn't said that!" I said.

"Don't encourage him please!"

"Hey! I am here," Rick interjected. "and I'll behave. I won't blow this, don't worry."

"Yes, we are doing a set, er, for an hour you said?" I asked Gary.

"Yeah. One hour. To finish the show."

"We are going to fine tune our high energy numbers, probably no ballads, we hope they might actually get off their arses and dance a bit. What do you think of a finish, which involved setting Rick's piano on fire?" (l hadn't mentioned this to Rick yet, but thought he'd love the idea.) Rick jolted up in his seat.
Gary looked worried, very worried.

"No, listen. We finish with Great Balls of Fire and we have a tray of lighter fluid on top of Rick's keyboard. Not much in it, just some pyrotechnic device maybe, that would light up on the last few bars.

"Fucking bonkers! Yeah!" Rick was on the edge of his seat.

"Oh dear." Gary sighed.

"No, seriously. We plan it to the last detail. We get the crew, and everybody involved to dance on our pianos for the last number, clear Rick's piano as Great Balls is being played, have a safety officer with an extinguisher standing by, and light up Rick's piano as he ends the last solo. It would be just for a few seconds but think of the effect. That's a wow factor isn't it?"

"We'll never get it past health and safety." Gary sighed.

"We don't tell them. We have everything checked and double checked with the fire chief, or someone similar, and the hotel's security. So, alarms don't go off. Think of the visual. It would be great!"

"Nervous now." Gary said, tapping his desk again. "I tell you what, do it, but you haven't told me ok? and for God's sake don't burn down the Dorchester."

Rick and I fist bumped.

"Man, when did you think of that?"

"Wanted to do it for ages, just never got around to trying it out."

"You can't put it in your set permanently." Gary said, shuffling uncomfortably in his seat. "Maybe the odd special occasion, we'll see, but get it tied down as tight as you can, and Rick, no jumping up and down in the flames…"

"Now there's a thought." Rick said cheekily.

"No! No! Don't even go there." Gary insisted.

"Just joking!" Rick said, winking at me. I didn't know if the wink meant he was just joking, or he really was thinking about it.

"Ok, I might pop down to Hemel tonight." Gary said. "Could do with getting out."

"Great. See you there." I said. "Come on Rick, let's leave Gary to do what he does best."

"Yep, cheers Gary." Said Rick, and we left to get some downtime before the Hemel gig.

We split, and Rick presumably went home. I did. I had a nice dinner with Yvonne and Ed, and a quick nap before getting changed for Hemel.

The usual one hundred, or so, metre queue greeted me at the entrance. It was so cool to walk straight to the front and be let in. Felt like VIP treatment.

"Hi Chris! Welcome back!"

"Yo man, wicked." Greeted me, as I made my way to the front. Some of the regulars had missed us both. It felt good. Inside, the smell of bleach hit me as final preparations were being made before letting the public in. Smokescreen was rifling through discs, and threw me the two fingered salute, without looking up, or changing his actions whatsoever. Rick was at the bar, with a gaggle of bar staff (all female of course) around him. On stage, Ray was building his kit. Very frugal, only one tom and one floor tom and a premier snare to die for. He'd tuned it and tightened it to perfection. It gave that hard 60s sound. An assortment of Zildjian cymbals completed the set. Paul was cleaning his bass. It felt like being a great night.

"Hi Christoff." Came from the girls, and a thumbs up from Rick. I acknowledged them and closed the dressing room door behind me. I just sat there in the peace and quiet and thought about the last week. What a stressful time. I was really looking forward to tonight. I wanted everything to be back to normal, whatever that was. The noise outside started to grow, as the place

started filling up. Smokescreen had cranked up the volume, and it felt like the night was beginning.
Rick was first in.

"Hi man." He said, with a cheeky look in his eyes. We bear hugged.

"You good?" He asked.

"Yep, looking forward to tonight, feel energised."

"Yeah know what you mean. Feels good to be back."

"Thanks man. Thanks for everything. I really do appreciate it. Everything. You're a true mate."

"That's ok buddy." I said, trying to release myself from Rick's enthusiastic bear hug grip.
Ray and Paul came in together.

"Yo!" They both announced.

"Hi guys." Rick said. "Ready for a blast?"

"Sure."

"Can we do that Monkees medley we used to do? I like the duelling bit on the end. If it vibes, we can keep it up for a while. Whaddya think?"

"Yeah sure Rick. Why not." I said.

We all nodded in agreement. We would do 'Hey Hey we're the Monkees', followed by 'Daydream Believer', followed by 'I'm a Believer', with an elongated ending, which tended to go on a bit, but worked every time. Rick and I alternating every 16 bars or so, until we found it running out of steam, then with a prearranged raised arm, we would end with that splat of a chord, usually climaxing the end of the first set.

Rick slammed his hand down on the keyboard, and we were off again. The Hemel crowd were jumping, in unison, it felt great. The Monkees went down well, with a seven-minute moment of madness on the
play - out. Rick was right, it worked really well, we should keep it in. Smokescreen worked them up further, the Hillbilly routines had mysteriously been dropped, thank goodness. It worked much better without them. The second half was great, and we left them shouting for more. I even spotted Gary making some moves. It was good to be back, after one of the worst weeks in my life.

Chapter 19

"Night darling. See you on Sunday, should be in time for tea."

"Night sweetheart, look after yourself and drive carefully."

I had tucked Ed in and said I would be away for a couple of days. This was met with a quivering pet lip, and I had to compare my time away with that of a ship's captain, or submarine captain, who could be away for months on end. He accepted this and realised my small stint away wasn't that bad after all. As usual, I couldn't sleep the night before travelling, as I was scared of missing the alarm, set for 3am. As usual, I always woke up a nanosecond before it actually went off. 02.58 I awoke and switched off the alarm, so as not to wake the others. No breakfast, nothing. Washed, dressed and out into the crisp, clean night air. Three hours later I was boarding the first flight out in the morning, nicknamed 'The Redeye', to Schiphol, Amsterdam. I felt a bit like an important businessman, not important I guess, but my business was music, and I wouldn't have changed it for the world. The other 'important' businessmen looked stressed, worried, and definitely unhappy. I was off on an adventure, a kind of paid vacation. My job wasn't work for me, and I had loads of downtime to have my coffee, and people watching; one of my favourite hobbies.

Schiphol, I discovered, had a very interesting history. It was built on reclaimed land from the sea. The Dutch were masters at this. There was even a famous sea battle, the battle of Schiphol, fought on the land where the airport is now. I made my way to the sex shop, next door to Maxime's, where I was playing, to pick up the key for the apartment, which was over the piano bar, right in the centre of Leitzaplahn. The whole area was such a hive of activity. Coffee shops galore, and architecture and canals to die for. I once played here on May 1st, Queen's day, a national holiday for everyone, which was taken very seriously by the very patriotic Dutch. Maxime's had hired a barge on the day and literally strapped a piano on the roof, and I played non-stop, travelling up and down the canals, advertising the bar. It was unbelievably brilliant. Every kind of watercraft was afloat, one had just six pallets strapped together, with an outboard put - putting it along, a single standing up 'Captain' with a crate or two of beer were the only occupants. Every boat imaginable, even a bright orange lifeboat, probably decommissioned from a large ocean-going liner, joining in the mayhem, and mayhem it was.

"Where do I pee?" I asked Klaus.

"In there," He pointed to the canal.
Everyone else was, so when in Amsterdam…….
"They open the gates, and a tide in and out cleans the whole canal system in one go." He assured me. Many times, we actually became gridlocked and they had to prise the boats apart with grappling hooks. All to rock 'n' roll. Quite bizarre.

I let myself in and went up to the apartment, which was in dire need of an upgrade, but the bedding was clean, and the whiff of the previous pianist's dope had nearly left. The two nights there were awesome. I had to play from 11pm until 4am. Quite a stint, and Klaus expected no breaks. There was an old car horn where the piano (a real grand in this case) joined the bar. One honk, and a beer, complete with a copious amount of froth, (or skum) as the locals called it, would come shooting along the bar, onto the piano, and I had to grab it before it went sailing past. Sometimes it did, much to the amusement of the crowd sitting at the piano, so close I could shake their hands. I nicknamed it the Black Hole of Calcutta. It filled up to beyond capacity too. My only break was forcing myself to the toilet and back. That could take a good ten minutes. Businessmen with obvious escorts for the night, would try to impress them, much to my delight, with large tips, often 1000 Guilders or Deutschmarks notes, (about £80) held over the tips bowl, for effect, and after my nod of gratitude, they would drop them in, and hoped it impressed their 'girlfriend.' The job only paid 1000 Guilders a night, about £80, but the tips would run into hundreds of pounds on a good night. It felt great in the apartment later, counting out denominations of currency and changing them up in the airport Sunday morning.

There was always the moaner at the piano too.

"I think you will find the second chord of Michelle is B-flat major, not minor." Said a young spotty upstart, so young, he was with his mother, who also moaned along with him.

"I think you'll find it's not." I replied and demonstrated playing said chord in major form. It was obviously wrong, but he wouldn't have it. Later on, his moany mother accused me of not really playing the piano, after I had played a blistering 'Let Me Entertain You', with its rapid, staccato piano stabs on the ending. I played it again, acoustically this time, without the backing track, and nailed it, much to the crowd's delight and roar, said mother and spotty Herbert left.

Rick had an equally busy time in Sheveningen, on the west coast. A vibrant town, busy in summer holidays with a superb beach and concrete pier. 'Crazy Pianos' is a large bar right on the Esplanade, but Rick was playing solo. Clubs often booked just one of us, if they knew it was going to be quiet. Makes a little bit of sense, saves money, but defeats the point of the concept, if you get my drift.

His flight came into Stansted very close to mine, so I waited, to give him a lift home. He came out of arrivals looking like he hadn't slept since he'd left on Friday.

He hadn't.

"Hi man." He growled, and we bear hugged.
"Wow Rick. You had a shower since you left?"
"Yeah, but not since yesterday. Bin up all night. Got involved in a shot race."
"Eh?"
"Well you know Ruben. We had a mad Saturday, went on till five. Then he gets out the tequila, not any tequila, only Clase Azul something or other, £300 a bottle, and we shot raced the whole fucking lot."
"Who won?" I already knew.
"Me, you dick. Who do you think? He collapsed after three quarters of it, so I finished it off, seemed a waste not to."
"It probably would have kept!"
"Nah, l couldn't bring it home, could I? Well I have, kinda." He said, patting his stomach.
"I don't know how you do it." I said, but I knew how he did it. He just did it.
"You?"
"Yeah Maxime's was bonkers. Klaus says Hi and the tips! Kinnel!"

I shook my hand as if in pain.

"Jammy sod. I got peanuts. There're all farmers out there." Protested Rick. Driving back, we chatted about the week ahead. Rick was in Roxy's again mid-week, then back to Holland. I was going to have meetings with Gary, regarding the Dorchester, then back to 'Amsters', which took us into November. I told Rick we'd be doing only Hemel until the Dorchester 'do', as we needed to be around to rehearse a special set for the big 'do'. Rick was cool with that, and said he was doing extra Roxy's, as the money was helping, but l think he was after Ms. businesswoman.

"I might pop down again." I said. More asking for approval, than a suggestion.

"Sure man. Great to see you. Why don't you do a set on your own. You'd love it and Steve will give you a couple of nights I'm sure."

"Nah, you do it, I'll come along and jam if that's ok. Love doing that. No pressure, just a bit of fun with my mate."

"Yeah. Any time."
Then Rick fell asleep.

I had a late Sunday lunch with Yvonne and Ed. Both busy telling me everything they had done, in chronological order, since I had left. I put Ed to bed. Not one gripe about his injuries, just pleased to have me back, and then I sat with Yvonne, for an evening of catching up on the sofa, her feet over my knees, relaxed and content. A wad of money on the coffee table, and that wasn't even my wages. Life felt good again.

    Rick was probably tying up Son, or having some kind of mad sex game with her, and all was probably good with them both too. Rick was comatosed, asleep, or unconscious, Son didn't know, or care, just glad to have him back too.
Son sitting on the sofa. Rick laying on Son, snoring.
The cat laying on Rick, purring and padding,

What could possibly go wrong?

Chapter 20

During the following couple of weeks, everyone went back to their routines. I helped with Ed's recovery, Yvonne returned to part time work, Rick and Son did their stuff. Gary did his. Rick and I had another routine weekend in Holland. Plenty of drink for Rick, not many tales of any wild women, maybe he was calming down, reigning it in perhaps.

Rick wasn't.

Thursday, Yvonne encouraged me to go out to see Rick at Roxy's.

"Go on." She said. "You've been great all week. Don't want you getting cabin fever."

"Ok, thanks." I said appreciatively. "I won't be home too late."

"Just enjoy yourself. I know you like Rick's jazzy set and you get to join in. It's good for you. Good for the soul."

"Thanks sweetie." I gave her a kiss on the cheek.

Strolling into Roxy's, Rick was on a break, sitting very close to Ms. businesswoman, hand on her leg.

"Hi mate."

"Yo Chris. Come and join us. This is Amburo." Rick enthused.

"Call me Amber, please." Amburo said, standing and shaking my hand.

"Hi, nice to meet you."

"What you having? Beer?" Asked Rick, standing, and moving towards the bar.

"Yeah sure. Budvar would be great."

"More Prosecco sweetie?" He asked Amber.

"Please. Love some." She answered holding Rick's hand.

Oh no, I thought. This was looking a bit serious. She was having the effect on Rick, that I'd seen before. She was extremely beautiful, sophisticated, intelligent, and very confident.

"Hi, I've seen you here before, fan of Rick's?"

"Yes, you could say that. Been coming here for a few weeks now. The guy can really play. You're not so bad too!" She winked.

"Thank you. I'll take that as a compliment."

"You're welcome." She smiled, a devastating smile.

"What do you do when you're not listening to Rick?"

"Oh, I work for the Somalian Embassy, in Whitechapel."

"Oh yeah? Is that where you're from? Somalia, I mean!"

"Yes, I am over here for a year. My father is the

Attaché here. So I've come out for the English experience, you know, improve my language and so on."

"Nothing wrong with that, I can assure you."

"Thanks. always room to improve, don't you think?" Her English was probably better than mine, I thought.

"Sounds good. Enjoying it here?"

"Yes, it's lovely, but so many people!"

"I know. I suppose you get used to it, living here." Rick returned with beers and bubbles. Amber went to the loo.

"Wow!" I said.

"I know!" Rick was on the edge of his seat. "Isn't she just drop dead gorgeous?"

"Yes, have to agree with you there."

"She's been here every week. Says she only comes on Thursdays to see me. We're getting on really well."

"Yes, I can see that! What about Son?"

"Shhhhh! Not now Chris. crickey, don't bring her up please."

"I won't, but I've seen you like this before Rick, and I think you're getting in too deep. She's only here for a year."

"I know. Four months left. Maybe I can visit her over there."

"Doubt it. I bet her Dad will be after your arse if he knew. Well you can't exactly take her home, can you? Tonight, or any night, I mean?"

"Hmmmm, l know, a car collects her at midnight.

Maybe you can do next Thursday for me, and I can take her somewhere else. Get her back here at midnight, no one will know."

"Rick! Please!"

Amber returned, put her hands on Rick's shoulders from behind, and kissed him on the back of the head.

"Thanks darling," she said, as Rick filled her glass. Oh no I thought. This was not going to end well.

It didn't.

Rick and I played a few more numbers. It wasn't so busy, and the crowd was quite mellow. I said 'Good Night' to the lovebirds and made my way home. Rick was making plans to meet Amber, inconspicuously somewhere, probably daytime, probably a hotel room, probably for wild sex. Well no probably there. Poor girl, I thought, although she looked like she knew what she was doing and obviously, genuinely liked Rick.

Sonja's suspicions arose from Rick's change in routine. He was out two or three evenings a week and went to Roxy's every Thursday. Sonja picked up on Rick's new 'vibe'. Something was going on, she thought. Rick showered more, shaved more, attended to his hair more. He was out a lot more, and came home really tired, and was not showing Sonja much attention. He told her he was doing two nights at Roxy's. He was really meeting Amber. She had told him she couldn't get involved, as her father was so strict, and that she'd be going home soon anyway, but she loved the sex, and the attention Rick gave her. Rick loved everything about her. To Rick she was exotic, erotic, and she gave his confidence a massive boost. Amber turned up at Hemel the following Friday. Rick was beside himself, now he could really show off and impress her. He was bouncing all over the dressing room before we went on stage. Ray and Paul noticed it and even asked him what he was on.

"It's lurrrrrve". He would say, and fiddle with his spiky hair for ages in the mirror. That night his jumps were higher, his voice growled more, and his playing was more blistering than ever. Rick had woken up. Something, someone, Amber I guess, had touched his soul, opened something, that he hadn't felt before. He was a new guy. Sonja had always told me he was a changed person after he'd met me and got in his teeth into serious playing. He was a changed guy again, according to my observations.

"Sonja is gonna know." I said to him in the dressing room, on our break. "Be careful, and don't hurt her Rick. Either run off with Amber, or pack it in. Don't mix it."

"She won't," he replied, "she's just happy to have me around."

"One-night stands are one thing, when it's obvious you don't give a toss about them, and maybe Son's ok with that, but this is different. You are different, and she'll notice that, and probably feel threatened. Be careful."

"Stop worrying, it's ok." He'd dismiss my protestations.

We went back and played a great second set. Ray was puffing more, pulling his snare closer, he was hitting it so hard, it kept moving away from him. Don't know why he didn't tape it down. This all made for great music, and a part of me was enjoying Rick's dalliances, Rick's new energy. I wasn't looking forward to the time the new girlfriend, was going to leave. Would he be devastated? Broken?, or go back to his, probably mundane for him, but secure, life with Son. The thought of him running off with Amber was unimaginable. Could I carry on with some lesser keyboard player by my side? Would I be good enough to carry the act forward? All of a sudden, I felt very vulnerable, and scared. We finished our set at 11:30, and Rick jumped off stage, and disappeared until five minutes past midnight. The car must have picked her up. He came into the dressing room, looking flushed, but content, a new purpose in him.

"And where have you been?" I teased.
Ray and Paul had left. I stayed behind, guessing Rick would return after saying goodbye to Amber.

"Disabled toilet," he said with a grin, "by the cinema."

"What?"

"Nobody uses it after the cinema is closed."

"What you took Amber in there?"

"Yeah, it's kind of extra naughty, if you see what I mean, and that baby changer thing is just the right height for__"

"Rick! Honestly. I can't believe it. You've been fucking her in there for the past half hour?"

"Yeah. She loves it. Gets fully naked and gets extra turned on when someone tries the door."

"But they probably need the disabled loo, and you're preventing them, poor things."

"Nah, there's others. Just something a bit more exciting doing it in there. Turns her on anyway."

"Fuck me Rick. You really are unbelievable."

"Suppose I am. Fancy a beer?"

Chapter 21

Monday morning, Rick and I met Gary in his office to discuss what would be required for the Dorchester.

"Right." Said Gary, making a bit of space on his desk, for a writing pad. "It's going to be on Wednesday, December 12th."

"Great! We don't miss a weekend's work." I said.

"No, never thought of that." Gary answered, "but Rank would probably have paid you for both, if it was on a weekend, as it is, their offering you both £500 for the day. There will be a full-dress rehearsal in the afternoon, then they will have a dinner for the VIPs, and the show will start about eight to eight thirty. Should be done by midnight. You also get a room each, keep it quiet, and food. All the artists will be fed in the Dorchester staff canteen."

"Great." I said. "Sounds good, Rick?"

"Yep. Cool, looking forward to it." He enthused.

"And free bar tabs also, but don't abuse it." Gary said the last half of that sentence directly to Rick.

"Don't worry Gary, it'll be ok."

"Good. Rank want a full show. There will be an MC. He'll do a bit of stand-up to warm them up a little, then a routine to be decided. They want Robbie to do a Freddie (Mercury) lookalike, and then you to finish off the show, and they want the highest energy, high octane, their words not mine, set you've got. No shocks, Rick__"

"I know! Don't worry."

"Just leave them wanting more, forty-five minutes should do it. Just do your best stuff."

"Got it." I said. "Leave it to us."

"Good. Can you let me have your set list when you've decided? Rank are interested in what you're going to play, so they feel a little bit informed, if the guests ask them anything."

"Sure thing. We'll get on with it. Pretty much know what it's going to be anyway. Right Rick?"

"Yeah, great balls of everything, I think."

"Ok." Gary stood up. "Anything you need, just let me know. Smokescreen wants to talk to you about the PA system and stuff, so give him a call. Can you sort that? Just get what you think you need, and run it by resources, they are expecting you."

"Great. I'll get on with that." I assured him.

"Coffee?" I asked Rick, on our way out.

"Sounds good." He skipped a little as we said our goodbyes to Jen, who immediately went into Gary's office with an armful of papers.

"Should be great this Dorchester do." I said as we ordered our flat whites.

"Yeah, looking forward to it." Rick was genuinely excited about the whole thing.

"Listen Rick, what are you doing about Amber? Son has been on the phone to Yvonne, just fishing, she reckons, but I've got a gut feeling she knows something, so be careful okay?"

"Yeah, don't worry. Amber's leaving after Christmas, so things will settle down then. Looking forward to a room in the Dorchester. I hope Amber can come."

"Rick…." I sighed, "might just be singles."

"No, I am going to ask for an upgrade. Four post bed maybe. I'll pay for the extra. That should impress her, I bet."

"Mate don't do it. She can't watch us. There is no place, and it's a private do, she can't just rock up and listen, like in Roxy's."

"I know, but there is before and after. She can start without me and be all ready and waiting when I go up."

"We'll be too busy, before, and I thought she was collected at midnight."

"No, she's going to tell her Dad that she is staying with a friend that night. Should be okay."

"Hmmm, got a bad feeling about it all." I said, trying to dissuade Rick, but he was adamant about a big night in a big posh bed, in a luxury hotel, with a posh 'bird', as he referred to her as.

"It'll be fine." He tried to reassure me. "Can't wait."

"Ok, whatever. I'm off. You in Roxy's Thursday?"

"Yep, and I've told Son I'm there Tuesday also, but I am seeing Amber really." Rick looked a little sheepish.

"Aw, Rick, please......."

"Don't worry. It's my business. Let me handle it."

"Jeez, unbelievable, just don't involve us. Yvonne won't protect you. She is more on Son's side if anything, and I'm not lying to Son for you, ok?"

"Sure, I get it. Don't worry it'll be fine, it's only for a couple of nights anyway."

"Yeah, well you know what I think."

"Ok. See you Thursday?"

"Yep sounds like a plan. Take care mate."

We bear hugged and Rick strutted off, probably to find Amber l thought.

Yvonne was home, cooking something delicious for dinner. Ed was ensconced on the sofa.

"Hi babe."

"Hi Dad."

"Hi guys." I answered. I gave Ed a kiss on his head.

"You good?"

"Yep, brilliant." He answered, ever defiant about his injuries.

"Hi darling." Yvonne came up behind me with a long warm hug, kissing the back of my neck.

"Steady!" I said.

"He he!" she giggled. "How did it go with Gary?"
We went to the kitchen and put the kettle on.

"Yep, all good. Got some sorting to do, PA and stuff. We have to do our best, high energy set for them. Rick's really onboard with it. They've given us a room for the night too, but I think I'll just come home."

"Oh darling, that's so sweet of you, but take the room, then you can have a drink and relax afterwards. Take it you've got a room each?"

"Yeah of course, Rick wants to upgrade his…" Then I stopped myself.

"What, for Son? That's decent of him."

"He didn't say. He was mumbling something about a four-poster bed or four post bed as he calls them."

"Oh well, good on him, Son will love that."

"Yeah well, don't say anything, in case it's a surprise."

"Of course not." She said with a cheeky smile.
If only she knew, and I felt bad that I was keeping a secret from her.

"She said anything else about Rick? Because he has been a little weird lately, but you know him..."

"No, she thinks he might be getting bored with her, he is less attentive and distracted, but she says the sex is still marvellous, well that's Rick, I said to her, and she just shrugged it off."

"Well I suppose it's their business," I said, "and I don't want to get involved, you know what they're both like."

"Puh, I know. I like Son, never been sure about Rick, but I know he is important to you, so I'll do my bit to support you with them both."

"Thanks darling. I think we just let them get on with their own thing, they both don't look too bad on it."

"Yes, you're right there. Just wish Son would put her foot down sometimes."

"Yeah, but you know Rick, he'd be off like a shot, if she tried to reign him in, and he keeps saying to me he's open with her about other women, and that Son puts up with it, as she'd rather have him around, than not."

"Hmm, I certainly wouldn't put up with that. Here's your tea."

"Go see Ed, he's missed you," she whispered.

"Hiya matey. Had a good day? Not hurting too much?"

"Hi Dad. Nah, it's okay. Just keeps itching and I can't get to it." He pointed to his plastered arm and mockingly scratched it frantically.

"Aw, never mind, soon have it off. Hopefully before Christmas, then you can rip open your pressies!"

"Yay!"

The diversionary theory worked again, thankfully. He was being so strong, and positive over everything. I hated to think he was in any discomfort whatsoever, and I longed for the day he was back to normal. Thank God, I thought, it could've been much, much, worse.

We ate dinner, put Ed to bed, and relaxed on the sofa. Yvonne with her legs over me, one of my favourite relaxing moments.

We both closed our eyes and fell fast asleep.

Chapter 22

Sonja put on her favourite bright red dress, lipstick, matching shoes, and headed out to Roxy's. It was Tuesday. Nervous, and not sure what was going on, she thought she would surprise Rick, and at the same time, quell her anxieties about him. It was probably nothing she would tell herself, over and over again, but the nagging doubt was eating away at her. Rick would be pleased to see her she thought, and she could marvel at Rick's playing, and enjoy Rick singing his jazzy, lovey, set to her, and to her only. All would be ok after a couple of drinks, and home with Rick afterwards for bonkers sex.

She thought it was a little quiet as she entered Roxy's, not many in tonight she thought, and the piano was closed.

"Hi Steve, Rick on a break?"

"Hi Son… Er…. no… Rick's not here tonight, it's Tuesday. Thursday is Rick's night. You okay?"

"Oh-I thought he was doing Tuesdays as well. Must've misheard him."

Shit, shit, shit, thought Son. Her mouth went very dry and it felt as if a knife had been twisted in her stomach, as the realization hit her. Where was he then?

"Drink?" Asked Steve, nervously, not knowing how to handle what was quickly becoming obvious to both of them.

"No thanks. - Oh, go on then, a JD and Coke please."

"Sure, and it's on the house." Steve said as he poured Son's drink.

"Oh, thanks." Son was on the brink of breaking down, and clumsily climbed onto a barstool, and nearly fell straight off again.

"You ok?" Asked Steve, handing Son her drink.

"I think so." She answered, swallowing half of the drink in one go.

"Rick not doing Tuesdays then? I thought he said he was doing some extra nights."

Son was shaking noticeably. Steve thought carefully, his brain racing for an answer, that would calm the troubled waters.

"No, just Thursdays. Haven't seen you here for a while."

"No, I'm a bit too tired to stay up so late."

Son's mind was racing like a train. She just wanted to run out of there, find Rick, take him home, and have everything back to normal. Steve, realizing what had happened, was also racing for something to say. Something to appease Son. Then he blurted out….

"We did talk about increasing the music nights here, and Tuesdays were mentioned, but look around."
Steve gestured with his arms, "It ain't too clever at the moment."

"Oh, I see." Son relaxed a little, but it still didn't explain this evening. "Did he come here to play, and you sent him home because it was quiet?"

"No, not this evening, but maybe I could try a few Tuesdays, see how they go."

"Ok. Thanks for the drink. I better be off." Son slid off the barstool and said good night to Steve.

"Yeah, you take care." Steve said, as he polished a glass, the same one he had polished for the last five minutes.

Son walked, almost ran, to the bus stop, fighting back tears, and trying not to throw up. Where was Rick? He often went out and came home late, but never before, she thought, had he said he was somewhere, and he wasn't. 1am, 2am, 3am, Son tossed and turned. Finally, she heard the door, and a few moments later Rick appeared.

"Where have you been?" Asked Son.
Rick could tell by the tone of her voice, that she knew something. The way she asked, suggested she already knew, and he better think quickly. He spotted the red dress over the bed end, and the shoes kicked off over by the window. She normally hung everything up, and

took care of her shoes, well her expensive ones anyway. Rick sat on the bed and said,

"Well I was supposed to be trying a few Tuesdays at Roxy's but I had too much in the Lion before I got there, and when I looked in Roxy's it was empty, couldn't even see Steve, so I went back to the Lion and can't remember much after that."

"Really?" Sonja asked, desperately wanting to believe him.

"Yeah, I think I did the right thing. I was really out of it, probably would have played shite anyway."

"You never play shite, Ricky". Sonja didn't know whether to tell Rick she'd been down to Roxy's, or to keep it quiet.

She kept it quiet.

For now.

Rick went to the bathroom and scrubbed himself clean.

Chapter 23

"Hi Yvonne."
"Hi Son, come in. You ok? I'll put the kettle on." Sonja wouldn't often cold call, but when she did, Yvonne suspected trouble, and this time she was right.
"How are you? Ed Ok?" Asked Son, taking off her coat.
"Yeah, he's on the sofa, go say hello."
"Hi big boy," Sonja said, sitting on the sofa, and giving Ed a hug, "how's it going?"
"Yeah, ok." Ed answered bravely and shuffled back into the sofa so Son could sit.
"I'm watching Mega machines, fire engines in this one, look".
"Yeah, great. I'm just going to have a cup of tea with your Mum. Want anything?"
"No thanks. Come and see me before you go".
"Ok, will do". Son kissed Ed on his head and ruffled his hair.
"Tea?" Yvonne asked, closing the door behind her.
"Yes please. That would be great."
"What's up?" Asked Yvonne, "you look upset."

"Oh, it's just Ricky. You know what he's like, I'm trying not to think about it but.."

"What? What's he done now?"

"Not sure. He's different. He's up to something. Well he's normally up to something or another, but this time, he's different. He told me he was doing another night at Roxy's and when I went down there to see him, well to check on him really, he wasn't there, just does Thursdays Steve said, and he was a bit nervous. So, I left, and Rick didn't come home till three, said he'd gone there early and there was no one there, well that was true, and that he was pissed in The Lion before, so he didn't go in, just went back to The Lion. I want to believe him, but it feels so wrong. He's up to something Yvonne, I know he is."

"Oh dear. How long are you going to put up with this Son? How long have you been run ragged with Rick's escapades? Come on, you're worth better than him. I think he just uses you as a base, and a safety net. You let him do what he wants. I couldn't do that with Chris. If he'd been messing around on that horrible night, I would have been off like a shot."

"I know. I know. I just love him, he's all I've got and I'm sure he cares really."

Yvonne was thinking of the double room, and hoping it was for them both.

"Well wait and see what Christmas brings. I'm sure you'll both be fine, but Son, if he is using you, get out, find a better man, they're out there and you're attractive, you'll easily find a Good 'un'."

"Oh, thanks Yvonne. I'm sure you're right. I'm just getting so depressed by it all, it's doing my head in."

"Hey, come on. You know Rick, he probably was pissed in The Lion, nothing new there, and at least he came home".

"Yeah, suppose so. Has Chris said anything?"
Yvonne thought carefully and said, "No, nothing special, you know those two, thick as thieves. He did talk to him, I asked him to, after that plastic doll episode, and what could have happened to Ed, and told him to tell Rick, to reign it in."

"Oh, Ricky was mortified about that."

"Yeah, but not his fault really, I should've had him better trained. Running off like that."

"Well you can't blame him, what a shock he must have had."

"I know, he was just too quick for me, and I got a bit of a shock too, I must say."

"Crickey, I bet you did, it must have been horrendous."

"It was, and you let Rick off with that one, or was it two he had, I don't know…"

"Oh, he said he was so drunk, he couldn't remember anything about it."

"Son!! Wake up please. Jesus, he must have known what he was up to."

"Yeah, you're right, I know, I'll just have to kick his arse a bit harder. Ok, I'd better be off. Sorry to land it all on you like this, just thought you might know something. Thanks for listening. Thanks for being my friend Yvonne."

"Oh, come here, give me a hug."

"A bear hug? Like those two do?"

"Yes, why not?"

"I'll just say bye to Ed, and hopefully see you soon. Do you know if we are invited to the Dorchester? Would be great to see Ricky play there."

"Don't think so. It's all private Chris said. Too many big knobs in. Think it's a very big deal for Rank."

"I know. Ricky is quite excited by it."

"Bye big fella." Sonja give Ed another kiss on the head and ruffled his hair. Ed gave his mum that rolling eyes look, that always made her laugh. She stifled a giggle, winked at Ed, and showed Sonja out.

"Oh, I like Son, and I don't really mind her pats on my head."

"That's nice of you to say so darling. Should we think about some tea? Daddy will be home soon, and I'm starving anyway. What do you fancy?"

"Ermmmm, sausage, beans, and chips."

"That's what Daddy always cooks for you. How about meatballs and spaghetti?"

"Yay! Great. Even better!"

Sonja went home and sat thinking about how to deal with Rick. Something was wrong, he wasn't the same, she was sure he was up to something. Should she say anything? Front him with Tuesday? Or wait and see what happens. She decided to wait. Maybe it was nothing, but it was eating away at her, and she hated it.

Rick came home, everything seemed normal.

"Fancy a snifter down at The Lion?" He asked. Sonja cheered up immediately, she wasn't often asked to join Rick in 'his' local.

"Yeah great. I'll put some lippy on!"

"Come on then, I could murder a JD"

All was good in Ed's household. He got his meatballs, his laughter at the dinner table, his carry up to bed, his night-time story, his tucking in, and all the love he could hope for. I kissed him good night and joined Yvonne on the sofa for 'our time'.

Chapter 24

We had the first meeting, regarding the Dorchester, in Gary's office. There would be a number of rehearsals, beforehand, and a final full-dress rehearsal on the morning of the gig. We would use the pianos from Hemel. Gary would see to that. He gave us each our orders. Smokescreen was to source a PA, a good one, no expense spared. He was on it, he said. Rick and I were to go through a couple of sets, and decide which one ran the best. Ted would oversee the Hillbillies (on fire!) and choose a suitable routine for the evening. Robbie would do his thing and deliver his Freddie Mercury lookalike, it was an awesome act, visually, and his voice was so realistic, you could actually believe it was Freddie, the band missing, although Robbie's professionally made backing tracks were perfect. Smokescreen would knit it all together in his own, inimitable way and hopefully the night should be a winner, with the allure of the Grosvenor, great food, and as much drinks as they want, the VIPs should have a fantastic time.

What could possibly go wrong?

"Any questions?" Asked Gary, giving me a look that I took to mean, 'don't mention the pyrotechnics'. Everyone seemed clear on what was needed, and we split and went our separate ways. On the way out I grabbed Smokescreen and asked if we could have Crown amps & JBL speakers and our usual Heath Allen mixer as that was what we were used to. I didn't want to start mastering a new PA on such an important night. He assured me he was on it, and had looked at hiring a ten-thousand-watt system. More for quality than volume. I knew I could depend on him, so that was one concern dealt with. The other was the pyrotechnics. Rick and I ordered our flat whites in Aroma and sat down for what were becoming regular business meetings, and I felt Rick was enjoying them immensely. He felt important and involved. He loved me asking his opinion on anything.

"So, what do you reckon to the pyrotechnics?" I asked him. How can we do it?"
Rick sat up excitedly.

"Wow what a great idea! I can't wait to do this one, stuntmen do it with gel. I could have it on my hands and they would look like they were on fire. It would be okay, because only the gel burns. It would only be for a few seconds, so I'll be okay, and think of the visuals!" Rick was learning a new language – 'corporate'.

"No! Absolutely not! I was thinking more of a tray along the top of the piano and maybe the leading edge, that would ignite only for a few seconds. Maybe some indoor fireworks material, it just has to ignite and last a few seconds that's all."

"Oh, how about petrol? It would have the desired effect and with the exact amount, it would burn out very quickly."

"Gotta think fire regs." I said. "Nothing too smokey or the alarms will go off, killing the sound and, will automatically dispatch half the London Fire Brigade."

"Ok, how about indoor fireworks stuff. There's a party shop in town that does that kind of stuff, let's drop in and have a look."

"Ok, sounds good, and we'll just see what works best, as a fast, pacey set. Ray and Paul might want to have some input on that, so we'll chat about it at Hemel on Friday."

"Just wing it shall we?" Asked Rick.

"Yeah, we could. Just see where the night takes us. I like doing it that way too, but think I we should plan this one a little more seriously, don't you think?"

"Yeah, you're right. I still want to start with 'Whole Lotta Shakin,' and of course save 'Great balls of Fire', till last with the piano on fire. Fucking ace!"

"Not the whole piano Rick."

"I know, I know. Only teasing!"

"Let's go down to that party shop sometime and see what they have. It's only four weeks away now."

"Can't wait." Rick said, eyes bright, and mischievous. A shiver ran right through me, I could see the headline in the Evening Standard, 'DORCHESTER HOTEL BURNT TO THE GROUND'. Oh no, mustn't let that happen.

Hemel came and went. It was always awesome to play there. It was our home ground and the fans were ours. We owned them. I managed to talk Gary out of sending us back to Brighton, I really couldn't face it, maybe in the New Year I would, but I didn't want to go back there at all. I would go to Roxy's to see Rick. Sometimes Amber would be there and they had their 'thing' going on. Sonja turned up one night, and scared the shit out of Rick. It was a sheer miracle that Amber didn't show that night due to an important dinner at the embassy, and her father insisted she attend. I tried to get Rick to at least decide one way or the other and not to fuck about with people's feelings like he was. He would just shrug it off, and say they had an understanding, but this was the side of Rick I didn't like at all. The next couple of weeks we all got into our routines, Hemel at the weekend, occasional Roxy's with Rick, (I still didn't fancy doing my own night, and just liked to chill with Rick, and not have any pressure.)

We were all Christmas shopping, and doing all that pre-Christmas buildup that folk do and Ed in particular was very excited. He was mending pretty well, the plaster was due off soon and hopefully he would be his energetic self again, although the injuries hadn't dampened his spirits at all. Rick was ducking and diving. I don't know how he did it. Sonja was going down fast. Yvonne and I talked to them both, separately, trying to help them but it was pointless. Rick was Rick, and Sonja didn't deserve Rick's dalliances. Son once came around to talk to Yvonne and she was hysterical, and distraught. She had found a love letter in Rick's jacket pocket. It was from Amber saying how much she loved Rick, but she had to return to Somalia soon, and she didn't want to hurt him, so she thanked him for giving her such a great time and making her experience feelings she had never had before. Yvonne had tried to placate her, and support her, but she told me she was seriously worried about Son's state of mind.

And she was right to be.

Chapter 25

"So how about this bad boy?"

Rick was holding up an indoor firework. It was a stubby little thing about an inch high and an inch in diameter. It had a bright covering on it and the words 'DAZZLER!' with lightning decals all over it and 'DANGER!' printed in red all around the base.
We were in the party shop.

"We could line a dozen or so on top of the piano. Light one and it would spread to the others and they would light almost simultaneously. Apparently, they just flare-up very brightly, and die straight away, hence the use for indoors. Just a flash with a few bright sparks and they're out. It would have the desired affect I'm sure." Rick enthused, eyes wild in excitement and wickedness. This wasn't too bad at all I thought, and then something suddenly occurred to me, this was a tad tame for Rick.

"You're not planning fiery gel on your hands, are you?"

"Eh!? No! Of course not. This will have the desired effect I'm sure, just a big flash at the end. Maybe we could synchronize a thunder flash at the same time……?"

"No. I think the flash will suffice."

"No," Rick mocked. "I think the flash will suffice." Rick said. shaking his head like a pendulum.

"Oi! Watch it!" I snarled at him.

"Could we try one of these?" He asked the shop assistant. We probably need a dozen or a dozen and a half."

"Yeah buy one and take it outside in the backyard and try it out. If you buy more, I won't charge you for that one."

"Okay. Let's go and check this out."

Rick paid £2.50, and we went out into the backyard. The little squib had a short fuse, which Rick reckoned we could twine together, setting them all off in rapid succession.

"Stand back!" Rick retorted and lit the fuse. A nanosecond later an impressive WHOOSH! And a blinding flash went about 3 feet into the air.

"WOW! That's sick!" Rick shouted.

I must admit I wasn't expecting such a performance from a little thing like that.

"Wow! Nice. I can see that working really well".

"Magnesium, I think." Rick explained. "With possibly iron filings for the sparks. No danger at all I reckon. Better turn off the smoke alarms for just a minute or two. Should be brilliant. Whaddya think, mate?"

"Yeah, does it for me," I agreed, "and it'll be visible right at the back. Should make 'em jump."

"Come on, let's go get some more." Rick was off, back into the shop.

"Can we have thirty of these please?" Rick asked.

"Thirty?" I asked.

"Yeah, we need to do a practice run, obviously."

I hadn't thought of that.

"And can you give us a discount on such a bulk buy?"

Rick was really turning corporate I thought, surely not.

"Yeah. Give me sixty quid."

"Great. Chris?"

Rick was looking at me, and then I realized it was for me to pay.

"Oh yeah." I paid the shop assistant, or probably the owner I thought, after such a discount.

"Can we use your yard again?" Asked Rick.

"Sure. Go ahead. Don't blow yourself up!" He joked. I followed Rick out, curious to see what he had in mind. Outside Rick took four of the little squibs out and twined the fuses together. Then he placed them in a line on the floor and ordered me to stand back.

"Can you take these over there, out of the way."

He handed me the remaining squibs, tightly wrapped in a bag.

"Right then. Watch this!"

Rick lit the first one and jumped back. A second later, four brilliant flashes, and a loud whooshing sound, confirmed that this was going to work, and work very impressively.

"Fuck!! That was bonkers!" Rick could hardly contain himself. We fist bumped and cleared up the empties.

"Thanks mate." Rick said, walking back through the shop.

"You're welcome." The owner said, happy with his sale.

"Coffee?" asked Rick, as soon as we were outside.

"Sounds good." and we headed off to Aroma.

"Man, that was bonkers. What a great idea. Why haven't you mentioned this before now?"

"Just something I've been toying with, and I thought we needed something extra for the big 'do'. I think it's brilliant. Well done tying them together like that, it really was impressive, can't wait to do it!"

"Me neither!" Rick said gleefully.

"Let's not tell anyone it's going to happen. Not even Ray and Paul. The shock on those two will have an added effect I think, and we'll just square it with the security person on the night. I'll bung him a twenty and say it's just an idea we have, and to disable the smoke alarms so they won't go off. We must have an extinguisher under the piano, just in case."

"Of course." Rick agreed. "Man, can't wait to do this. If it goes well, we could do it in Hemel. Run it by Craig, he'll see it in the Dorchester anyway. As long as the hotel doesn't burn down it should be great."

"Let's see how it goes first. One thing at a time."

We drank our coffees. There was an extra buzz in the air this time. Caffeine and gunpowder, or magnesium maybe. Rick was tapping his legs double-time, hardly containing his excitement. I suddenly had a really good feeling about this. Rick was into it, and enjoying it. I felt so pleased for him and couldn't stop smiling. The following days we met with Gary and Ted plus some of the bigwigs from Rank. "Orifice tossers!" Rick would call them, a nice play on words I thought.

We would meet at Hemel during the daytime, and run the whole evening, perfecting this and perfecting that. Ted 'choreographing' Hillblillies On Fire. They were doing 'Tailfeather'. Ted's impression of a bird with a tail feather was quite hilarious, or very sad, according to Rick. Robbie's, Freddie was spot on, and Smokescreen's warm-up got funnier every time he did it. Plus, he played some great grooves to get everyone moving. The evening was beginning to shape up nicely, and I was loving my secret ending, that I knew would just put the icing on the cake of a great night. Rick would nudge me at the exact time the fireworks would start, and once again I couldn't contain my smile. I am sure at one point, Gary noticed, and second guessed us, as he gave me a very knowing look. Maybe I just imagined it, as he never mentioned it once.

Chapter 26

Sonja paid the shop assistant and put the newly bought Stanley knife into her handbag, said thank you and left the hardware shop.

We, meanwhile, were very busy in the Dorchester. An events company had been employed to build a Jumping' Jacks background, complete with stuffed beavers and similar artefacts. They had built it all offsite, and were now frantically assembling it onto a stage which has two brand-new, bright red, mock grand piano frames, intended for Leeds, a new venue soon to open. Ten thousand watts of Crown amps and JBL speakers stood either side of the stage, looking quite mean I thought. Sleeping giants, waiting to be woken, and growl into life. A cacophony of sound rang around the ballroom, sanders, nail guns, sawing, banging, and the occasional screaming of orders, and plenty of blasphemies. Some of them were very amusing.

"Woah! Hemel all over again!" Exclaimed Rick.

"Looks good." I said. "It will be done for tonight, it always is." I assured him.

Gary came rushing over.

"Glad to see you two." He puffed. "Can you sort out your sound, and we can sound check. Everything seems to be on track. Wish I hadn't said that. We've been here since midnight."

"Wow! I'm impressed. Sure, we'll get on with it."

"Anything you want, ask Roger over there, the guy in the red T-shirt with 'THE BOSS' on the front".

"Okay. Will do."

We made our way to the stage, and began setting up. A large box of every cable imaginable was centre stage. We started digging out what we needed. Two brand-new Roland stage pianos were on top of the grand piano frames, still in their polythene wrapping. We unwrapped them and placed them into the gap where the original keyboard for the Grand piano would have been. They fitted perfectly.

"Great! Love it when a plan comes together." I said to Rick.

"Yep. Don't speak too soon, but must admit, I've got a good feeling about all this." Rick was beaming.

"Oh mate, well done you. Thanks for being a pro."

Rick loved any appreciation. I learned to give it generously, as it reassured him of his worth. Something he fed on, and I wanted him content, and stable. He played so much better when he was appreciated. We busied ourselves, plugging in lead after lead, searching for electrical extensions, switching things on to check them. All seemed ok.

Smokesceen breezed over, and said whenever we were ready, we could run a song, and fix the sound. Joiners, and electricians, were bustling around us. Loud beeping coming from the cherry pickers, as lights were assembled above our heads, on frames of crisscrossed metal, similar to that of a tower crane. Ray and Paul turned up, together, bang on time. Typical I thought.

"Yo!" Rick shouted.

"Hiya!" they answered in unison.

I couldn't contain a smile.

"There is a back line all ready," I said pointing to a drum kit and a Marshall bass stack.

"Great!" Said Ray. "I've got my own snare, so I'll just swap them and get everything else where I want it."

Paul had his trusted Fender with him. It was the most beaten up, scratched, faded, guitar I had ever seen, but what a sound. So warm, and sometimes so heavy, you could feel it hitting your chest. They set to, getting their stuff together and we were soon ready to do a sound check. Notes from the pianos were clear and solid through the PA.

"Turn those off!" Rick shouted to smokescreen, pointing to the two large monitor speakers, facing back at us. I so agreed with him on that one. We wanted to hear what was going out to the floor, not what was being fed back to us, through the monitors, as it could be a completely different sound altogether.

"That ok with you two?" Rick asked Ray and

Paul.

"Yeah great. We certainly can hear you well enough!" Ray puffed. Smokescreen went through his sound check routine. Ray first, one drum at a time. Smokescreen fiddling on the mixing desk. First maximum bass, then maximum top, eventually working them back to a clear, crisp, but warm sound.
Paul played his bass, fiddled with his sound and he and Smokescreen gave each other a thumbs up when the sound was just right. Ray and Paul then played together, and Smokescreen put a thumbs up and shouted,

"Great! Thank you."
Rick went next, he had already set his sound on his Marshall Stack, Smokescreen just had to take it, as is, out through the mixer, and set a general level. Having the Marshals behind us meant we didn't need the monitors. The vocals came out well in front of anything else, thanks to Smokescreen's expertise, and it all gelled together beautifully. I went next, and in no time we were ready.

"Ok to run a sound check?" Came thundering out of the PA everyone jumped, but put their thumbs up.

"Yeah? Great. Off you go guys," ordered Smokescreen. Rick said nothing, just started 'Whole Lotta Shakin', that beautiful walking bass, with offset syncopated chord stabs. I joined in, causing a 'phasing effect', doubling the sound, and then thickening it. Sixteen bars in, and Ray and Paul came in right on cue.

We were thundering along. Everyone stopped what they were doing and stared at us. Smokescreen was bent over the mixer doing his stuff, and soon I felt the sound settle into a glorious mix of organized chaos. Rick was controlling everything. The tempo wasn't quick, as we normally did it. He was cruising, listening intently to everything. Ray and Paul give assuring nods. I settled in for the ride. Rick sang and it came out crystal clear. We instinctively took a solo each. Nothing too long this time. Rick signalled with his raised arm, and we finished the number well short of how we usually played it.

"Brilliant." Shouted Rick.

Spontaneous applause broke out from the workforce. Big smiles, thumbs up, plenty of whoops, and they got back to work.

"All good?" Asked Smokescreen as he wandered over to us with his trusted gaffer tape, and started fixing cables to the floor, so as to reduce the trip risk. Health and safety requirements.

"Yep. Brilliant." I said.

The others agreed, there was a buzz on the stage, an energy I'd felt many times before. This was going to be great. Rank would have their success. We would get recognition and promotion, and life would be sweet.

Or so I thought.

Smokescreen went through his routing and rehearsed the Hillbillies. Rick sticking his fingers down his throat, luckily nobody noticed. Robbie took a number, and for a minute or so it sounded like Queen were really on stage.

"Hungry?"

"Er… Yeah." Came back from the others.

"Let's go and find that staff canteen." I said. The food was good. We just asked the chef to give us what was going. A choice between pasta or roast beef. We tucked in, like only musicians can, and scoffed the lot.

"I'm just going to sort out my room." Rick announced.

"Okay see you later. Back here at six for some dinner?"

"Yeah sure. Cool." And Rick was off.

"Room?" Asked Ray and Paul.

Shit, I thought, think quickly.

"Yeah, you know Rick. He's got this really posh 'bird', he wants to impress, so he's booked a room with a four-poster bed, or four post bed as he calls them, probably blown his fee, and the rest, knowing what this place costs."

"Wow!" Said Ray. "Plonker."

"Heard it all now." Added Paul.

Phew. Got away with it, better not let out I've got a room too. Don't know why they couldn't have given them one. They were worth it. I hung out with Smokescreen for a while, watching it all come together.

Final touches were added here and there. Roger 'the boss' shouting this, and shouting that, in a good commanding way, not arsey at all. I'm sure some of the paint would still be wet when we opened. Some of it was.

Rick took his room key from reception and excitedly made his way to the lift.

"Wow!" He exclaimed when he entered. It was massive, he thought. A large four poster bed, with white lace around the top, and sides. More pillows than he'd ever seen in his life. Champagne on ice.

"What!" He exclaimed to himself. A large fruit bowl filled with fruits he didn't recognise, maybe Amber could show him how to eat them, and a bunch of expensive, exotic, giant white lilies in a vase, big enough for a dozen goldfish. That's how Rick measured vases. A sofa, bigger than his and Sonja's bed at home, covered in dark green velvet, pulled tight with matching buttons, and again covered in a plethora of cushions. Rick placed his ghetto blaster beside the bed on the bedside table, making sure the speakers were at the same height as his ears would be. He had brought two CDs, both Tchaikovsky. Swan lake and the fourth Symphony. "The most perfect piece of music ever written", he would say to anyone who would listen. He was referring to the fourth. It's a staggering piece of music, sometimes known as the 'fate' symphony, dedicated to a woman, Tchaikovsky had never knowingly met, who would send him money to support his composing. She was in the audience on the first airing of the symphony in St Petersburg, and Tchaikovsky knew this, but still they never met. Not to my knowledge anyway.

Rick felt the sheets. Smelt the pillows. Checked out the bathroom. "Bonkers" he kept saying. He'd arranged to meet Amber outside the entrance at 2 pm, and there she was.

"Wait till you see this!" He enthused and took her by the arm and led her up to his room.

"Nice." Said Amber on entering, looking around, and taking it all in. "Why thank you." she added, throwing her arms around Rick.

Rick carried her to the bed, and almost threw her on it.

"Whoa! Hang on, we've got all day and night!"

"I know. Just want to lay here with you a while. Isn't this great? Look - champagne!"

"Hmmmm love it. Save it for later?"

"Yeah sure. Come and see this."

Rick led her to the bathroom and immediately turned on the Jacuzzi.

"Come on, let's have some of this, with the champagne, and I'll get some more for later."

"Ok sweetie. Whatever you say." And Amber started undressing. Rick couldn't believe his luck.

Sonja entered the Dorchester and headed for reception. In her hand she had an envelope with a good luck card in it for Rick, for tonight.

"Hello", she said to the receptionist, "Can I leave this here for Rick, Er, Richard Morelidge, he is one of the pianists working for Rank. I just wanted to wish him good luck."

"Sure. I'll see that he gets it."

"Thanks very much, bye."

As Sonja turned to leave, she paused slowly, looked back and saw the receptionist pigeonhole the letter into the slot marked 505. Sonja knew Rick was seeing someone, and guessed he was bringing her here as he was so definite about Sonja NOT coming. She was at the end of her tether and was about to show Rick a lesson he'd never forget, a revenge he couldn't possibly imagine.

Chapter 27

We were 'backstage' at the Dorchester, in a makeshift dressing room, in one of their private dining facilities. I could hear the room starting to fill. The noise increasing as the guests entered, found their places, and ordered their drinks. A general ambient noise increased and there was a buzz in the air. The guests did not quite know what to expect, I'm sure, hence the anticipation was very high. Dinner was served, and a quick peep confirmed a packed dining room, with waiters scurrying back-and-forth, serving the VIPs their every wish. Smokescreen's music gently playing in the background, 'acoustic wallpaper', l used to call it, having its desired effect. I had seen the security guard on stage and gave him his twenty. He rolled his eyes and said, 'Don't fuck it up.'

"So," I said to Rick, "Amber upstairs?"

"Yeah, she's waiting for me. Got an all-night pass from the embassy. Man, you wanna see the room, it's bonkers."

"I bet, must have cost you a fortune."

"And the rest, but worth it."

"Aw mate, sort this out when she goes back, please. It's very stressful for us, you know. We love Son, and we don't like what you're doing. It includes us too you know."

"I know I'm sorry, one last time that's all. I'll make it up to her at Christmas I promise."

"Do that will you, and try to knock it on the head. When we open Leeds, bring Son with you, she'll love it, and you'll have to rein it in then."

"Ok. I get it. Leave it to me."

I thought Rick really meant it. Something about his eyes. He loved Son and didn't like what he was doing, but he couldn't help himself. I thought, at last he was starting to try. We would see. The room resembled a dressing room at a football match. Ray and Paul sat together chatting. Robbie was reading his book. The Hillbillies were going through their routine, tweaking moves here and there. Gary would pop in now and again to make sure we were okay and, like I said, the anticipation was growing. A sudden surge in volume from the dining room, raised it to another level. Smokecreen was in his place. The chatter from the guests died away, and the bass came through the walls. Smokescreen was in his element.

"Good evening everyone." He announced, fading the volume every time he spoke.

"We've a really exciting evening for you all tonight… Thank you for coming, and I hope you're all enjoying the hospitality provided by Rank…… Thank you Ted!" He pointed to Rank's table and Ted stood up soaking up the dopamine, and the applause, he thought it was only for him.

"Sad git." Rick mumbled.

A muffled snorting went around the dressing room.

"We have a great evening's entertainment for you tonight", continued Smokescreen,… "A new concept in nightclub entertainment, that Rank have put together in a number of venues, that have exceeded all expectations… and we are rolling out more as I speak… Leeds will be next and there are plans for many more… It's a great way to utilize old spaces, bring long dead buildings back to life. We've invited you all here so you can buy into this franchise, and enjoy the success in your own businesses… Rank will help you build your own venues, and guide you through the process, our expertise will save you thousands on set up costs, and getting it just right will ensure your success."

"Ted didn't write this, surely." Rick said, head in hands. Another stifled laugh went around the dressing room. Smokescreen went on persuading the guests that this was better than sliced bread. He told a few anecdotes, jokes, including my favourite,

"Have you had the world's shortest blues song?"

"Didn't wake up this morning……"

He sang the punchline. They loved it and laughed out loud, applauding every gag and even started 'hooting and hollering'.

"First of all, tonight we have, 'The Hillbillies on Fire', a great country and western act, I am sure you're going to love."

The Hillbillies suddenly jumped up and waited by the door, for their cue.

"Acts like these give a feel-good factor out to the audience, brightening up their day, and putting smiles on faces…"

I managed to kick Rick just in time, as he was about to put his fingers down his throat in distaste. Ray and Paul noticed, and couldn't stop smiling

"So, Ladies and Gentlemen, please give it up for…'THE HILLBILLIES ON FIRE'!!"

The hillbillies duly shot out of the door, and Shake a tailfeather started. The audience clapping enthusiastically.

"Really?" Groaned Rick.

"Shush, it's not all about us."

"Oh man, it so is." Rick meant it.

Tailfeather finished, and in burst The Hillbillies, sweat soaked, and beaming from their five minutes of stardom.

"Weren't they great?" enthused Smokescreen, "it's a brilliant way of using bar staff, and utilizing their hidden talents, it gives them a sense of purpose. You will have no shortage of volunteers to fill these roles. A good economic move too..."

The music rose and faded as Smokescreen read his script.

"And now Ladies and Gentlemen …"

Robbie jumped to his feet, hopping from foot to foot, psyching himself up for his moment. God, he looks so like Freddie, even had a real moustache. He must've gotten some weird looks on a night out in the pub!

"The world of lookalikes is growing...."

Now the music had stopped as Smokescreen delivered his introduction. "Rank have used Elton Johns, Rod Stewarts, Tina Turners, Michael Jacksons...."

(The best Michael Jackson lookalike was a female, and she was opening Leeds with us, I was looking forward to that, she was awesome.)

"But tonight, we have a very special one, selected just for you all. We hope you can escape.... believe…..enjoy…..the amazing…….

FREDDY MERCURY!!……"

Robbie shot out of the door, to the opening bars of 'Crazy little thing called love'. A good choice, it would lead nicely into our rock 'n' roll set. Robbie pranced, and used all of the stage, really connecting with the audience, they were loving it, lost in the fantasy, to them it was really Freddie. He was that good. Robbie finished and was taking his bows when suddenly the next track started. Robbie had given Smokescreen his Minidisc of his set and merely said 'play track seven', as soon as it had stopped, track eight started, as it would have done in his set. An amazing piece of professionalism happened next. Smokescreen didn't cut the track, Robbie instantly went into 'The Great Pretender', and it ran seamlessly. Nobody noticed, except us of course. The audience loved it. Robbie with his invisible vacuum cleaner and as much camp as he could muster, without overdoing it. Smokescreen was ready this time. As soon as the track stopped, he ejected the disk, and Robbie once again took his bows, and ran off stage, high-fiving Smokescreen,

"Whoa! Well done!" We all said, as a sweaty Freddie Mercury, (you had to be there) bounced into the dressing room.

"Forgot to cancel the bloody autoplay." He complained, but I think he enjoyed the extra song.

"And now Ladies and Gentlemen the highlight of the evening. An exciting new concept in musical entertainment. They have this in the States, and it is proving to be a money-spinner, and a growing phenomenon. We crept onto a dark stage, a single spot picking out Smokescreen. Hopefully no one noticed us, although we were very close to the tightly packed dining tables with their little lamps, in the centre of the tables. Rick had the pyrotechnics on the floor all tied together waiting to go.

"So, ladies and gentlemen, strap yourself in, and enjoy……. THE DUELLING PIANOOOOOS……"

The audience clapped enthusiastically as Rick started his walking bass into 'Whole Lotta Shaking'. I had instructed the lighting engineer not to push up the lights until the bass and drums came in, I thought it would add to the anticipation. Sixteen bars in and I joined in. Once again thickening the sound. Smokescreen pushing up the volume ever so slightly.

Then Rick changed everything.

He looked intently at Ray and Paul, as if to say, 'wait a minute'. They instantly got it. The vibe was amazing with just the two of us. The audience started clapping, and on the wrong beat, Rick was focused and didn't really object. After another thirty-two bars or so, Rick raised his arm and shouted '1234' and Ray and Paul came in right on cue. The lighting engineer instinctively got it too, and the lights exploded into life, and we were off. The audience jumped to their feet, dancing, and clapping. Rick started singing and we were once again motoring like a train. Smokescreen made some adjustments to the sound, and I was in heaven. We took solos each. Rick was outstanding. I played catch up but held my own. Ray puffed. Paul bounced. Song after song, we rattled through our set.

Rick was such a pro, no gaps between songs, just relentless hammering of pianos and general mayhem on stage. Some of the VIPs were now dancing on tables. Wow I thought. These were just the VIPs. The kids are going to love it even more. Then our last number, and the big finish. Rick started 'Great Balls of Fire'. This time, I couldn't hide my smile.

Then I couldn't believe what happened next.

"What?" Shouted Rick. "Fuck. No…" Luckily off mic.
"Eh?" I said, wondering what had alarmed Rick so much. Ted, in his infinite wisdom, had gone into the dressing room and ordered The Hillbillies to dance on top of the pianos. They'd never done this before, but the audience were encouraged to at our regular gigs. Rick elbowed me in the back and said,
"Shit, look."
They came bouncing out onto the pianos, and were giving it their all, jiving, clapping, and 'Hillbillying'. Rick grabbed the leg of the nearest one and signalled him to get down. This was met by a big smile and a thumbs up. Obviously, he didn't get the message at all. Rick grabbed again, and shouted,
"Get the fuck off the piano". Luckily his mic was off, (I had taken over the vocals) but I still heard him. Another smile from the Hillbilly and another thumbs up.

"Keep going". Rick screamed to Ray and Paul.
Rick grabbed a third time, really hard, I heard the "OW!" Rick held up the pyrotechnics and signalled frantically to him to get down. It must have looked like a bomb, because all of a sudden, the Hillbillies vacated the piano and ran screaming into the dressing room. Rick raised his arm, and we finished our last eight bars. Ray and Paul got it. I got it, and we ended with that big splat of a chord. Rick lit the fuse, WHOOSH! Several times in succession, a blinding flash of brilliant white light. Ray nearly fell off his drum stool but kept playing. The audience gasped, and stood clapping like crazy. We had finished and were taking our bows. No alarms went off. The Air con sucking out the smoke. Ted's face was in total shock. Not sure if he was furious or just plain shocked.

"More! More!" Came from the audience, but we wanted to leave them hungry, and left the stage.

"Ladies and Gentlemen; Duelling Pianos."
Smokescreen put on some quiet grooves and came bursting into the dressing room.

"What the……? That was awesome."
Ted came in. Gary came in. The Hillbillies from Rick's piano were traumatized.

"We thought we were done for," one of them complained.

"YOU!" Ted Pointed at Rick, blood red with rage.

"Whoah Ted." Gary grabbed his arm. "That was genius. Listen to them."

The crowd were stamping in unison to, 'we want more, we want more.' It was like the dressing room in Hemel. Ted was lost for words and stormed out.

"Don't worry, he'll be okay." Gary assured us.

"You guys ok?" Gary asked the Hillbillies.

"Yeah, sorry about that." Rick apologized to the one he was grabbing, "I just had to get you off there."

"It's ok, just wish you'd told us."

"Well I never expected you to come out like that. It was a good idea actually. Even if it was Ted's."

"Right." Gary said. "Chris, Rick, come with me, I want you to do some networking. Come on."

Rick grabbed a Budvar and downed it in one.

We went out to cheers and backslaps. Rick took a drink off every table. We 'networked' the crowd and tried to convince them to buy the concept. We didn't need to. Ted had been told by many, they wanted in, and contracts could be sorted out the following day. A big success. So very nearly a big disaster. I thought Rick might light the fireworks anyway, even with the people still on the piano. I was so glad he got them off first.

"Kinnel!" Rick said, as we were back in the dressing room. "I couldn't believe it. I even thought of holding them up in the air, but they were too flimsy. Should've had them on a board, or something. I never expected that to happen. Jeez!"

"I nearly died! I thought you would just light them regardless."

"I did think of that! "Well, it worked, it was bonkers. Must do that again."

"We'll see. Gary did a good job sticking up for us. I think Ted will be ok, it's all about numbers and I think they'll be getting them!"

"Hope so. Bear hug buddy." and we bear hugged.

"You got somewhere to go?"

"Do you mind.? I've been looking forward to this. She's waiting for me in bed, or in the Jacuzzi!"

"Ok Rick. Off you go. See you at the debrief tomorrow 12 o'clock remember, in the bar."

"Oh yeah, I'll be there."

"Have fun and be careful."

"I will."

Rick was out of the door.

I went on stage and helped clear up. Ray and Paul had packed away and were saying their goodbyes.

"What was THAT?" Ray puffed.

"I know, pretty bonkers hey?"

"One day he'll come a cropper." Paul added.

I hung out with Smokescreen. The guests were filing out slowly. Some were still sitting, talking intently.

"Well. That was fun." Smokescreen said, wrapping a cable around his arm.

"Nearly didn't happen." I said, "Bloody Hillbillies were really, nearly on fire!"

"Ha! Yeah. That'd worked."

We laughed out loud.
An army of people swarmed in and 'the boss' started shouting his orders.
We left them to it and went to the bar for the after party.

"Anyone home?" Rick asked.

Amber giggled from the bed.

Sonja entered the Dorchester and headed for reception.

Chapter 28

"Hi, 505 please." Sonja gave the receptionist her best smile, and hoped she wouldn't become suspicious.

"Name please?"

"Morelidge. Mrs. Sonja Morelidge." This worked, as Rick had actually checked in as a Mr. and Mrs. Morelidge.

"There were two keys issued when you checked in. Have you lost one, because I'll have to issue two new ones for security reasons."

"No, no. I changed handbags before I went out, and it's definitely in there. Silly me." Sonja giggled, and tried to disguise her shaking.

An elongated oh-kay from the receptionist, as she typed something out on her keyboard and took a blank key and ran it through a reader, to enable it to open 505.

"There you are, Mrs. Morelidge, have a good night."

"Thank you." Sonja took the key and headed towards the lifts.

"Mrs. Morelidge?"

"Yes?"

"It's that way, the lift in the far corner."

"Oh, silly me!" Sonja played the dizzy blonde to perfection.

"Only been here once, it's quite overwhelming isn't it. Probably never get the chance to stay here again. Thanks very much." Sonja shrugged her shoulders, giggled again, and headed towards the lift. The Receptionist picked up the phone to call 505, but changed her mind when Sonja shrugged her shoulders and gave her, her best smile just as the lift doors were closing. It was very late, and Mr. Morelidge might not want disturbing. So, she let it go. Put it down to young love. After all she had noticed she was wearing a wedding ring. She didn't know it was one of Sonja's dress rings, with the Tanzanite turned around so only the band was visible.

Sonja stepped out of the lift, and immediately could hear the dulcet tones of the fourth symphony coming through the air. It wasn't too loud to disturb the guests, but she knew what Rick was up to. She moved nervously past 501, 502, 503, 504, and finally 505. The music was more audible now. She slid the credit card key into the lock and pulled it out. The red light turned green and a ping confirmed the door was now unlocked. Slowly, so slowly, Sonja pushed open the door, just enough to peep inside, then jumped out of her skin, as a door further down the corridor opened and someone put out the room service empties, for collection, making a loud clanging sound. The door snapped shut.

Sonja composed herself, took a deep breath, then used the key again. The red light turned green, another ping and once again Sonja slowly pushed open the door a fraction of an inch, just enough to see what looked like bodies under the duvet, obviously in an erotic state. The music swelled up louder, and Sonja quickly entered, closed the door, and laid down on the floor. She wriggled commando style, behind the sofa. She gathered her senses. The music was quite frantic, and the noises coming from the bed ebbed and waned, with Tchaikovsky's passions. She dared a peep from behind the sofa.

"Thought so, you little bastard." Thought Sonja. She resisted the urge to stand up and shout out, she had a much better plan, and much bigger punishment for Rick, "and a four-poster bed just like you always promised me. Perfect Ricky. Perfect."

Sonja jumped out of her skin when the final movement started. It always made her jump, even when she knew it was coming. She gulped some JD from her hip flask, to steady her nerves. The urge to yell, was storming around inside her, fuelled by that last movement.

"Concentrate Son, concentrate." She whispered to herself. "You've only got one shot at this."

Most of this movement was very loud, very frenetic, very powerful, and Sonja had no problem crawling under the bed unnoticed, which to her relief, had four legs and enough room to get underneath easily. Once under, she gathered her thoughts. No change from the bed. The girl was very vocal, and Rick made it obvious how he was doing. Sonja opened her handbag and took out the four pairs of pink velvet covered handcuffs. One by one she attached them to each leg of the bed. Luckily, she thought, the legs were just thin enough for the handcuffs to go around. She turned over to lay on her back.

Another shot of the JD. She was still shaking.

Tchaikovsky was blistering along, as were the two lovers, just inches away from Son's face. A lull in the music. Sonja had to act quickly, not long left now, she thought, as Tchaikovsky went into his grand finale. Bold brass, blasting from Rick's ghetto blaster, made you feel you were actually at the concert. Sonja handcuffed her left leg into the handcuffs on the bed leg and snapped it shut. She did the same to her right leg, a satisfying click as it too, snapped shut. She took out the Stanley knife very carefully, as it had Rick's fingerprints on it. Son had made up a story of a picture she wanted framing, and Rick had cut out the inlay for her. She then positioned the right-hand handcuffs in a way so that it was open with the opening facing towards her, carefully standing it vertical as opposed to it lying flat. She practiced a few moves with her arm, drawing it across her chest towards the open handcuffs, stopping it just short of the opening. When she was satisfied, she took one last swig of the JD, finishing it, and tossing the flask towards the end of the bed. She then set her left hand into the third handcuff and snapped that shut too.

She was ready.

She had to act quickly and precisely, as the music was reaching its climax. So was 'the girl', thought Sonja.
 "You bastard Ricky, have some of this."
 Sonja took the Stanley knife in her right hand. She looked at the open handcuffs and mentally practiced what she was going to do. Rick and Amber were climaxing. Sonja just wanted to scream, and scream, but she held it in, amazingly. She took a deep breath, and with absolute determination, she carried out a move she had rehearsed many times before. Gripping the Stanley knife's, blade towards her, she held it against her throat, and with one single movement, sliced it open, and slammed her hand into the fourth handcuff. It snapped shut, just as she had planned. The Stanley knife went sliding over the floor and disappeared behind the curtains. Sonja had just a split second to see it was complete. She almost smiled as the blood pumped out of her, hitting the underside of the bed.
 "Oh Ricky." she thought "What are you.........."

And she was gone.

The music stopped. Dead quiet.

Amber and Rick laid gasping, holding each other tightly, getting their breath back.
"That was amazing Ricky. Wow. Where am I?"
Neither of them noticed the pool of blood, creeping out from under the bed. There were pints of it. Sonja had stopped fitting. The blood had stopped pumping, and all three lay in an eerie silence.
A silence that was so serene, two lovers recovering from their orgasms, one lover at peace, forever.
The silence lasted quite a while, the two blissfully unaware what lay beneath them. Until Amber needed the toilet.

"AAAARRRGGGHHH, NOOOOOOOO.....RICKY, RICKY"

Amber screamed like a savage beast, like a wild boar caught in a trap.

"LOOK! LOOK!" She screamed hysterically, pointing to the floor, her legs now covered in blood, as she was trying not to stand in it, as if she was on hot coals, but this only made the blood splatter more.

"What the…?" Rick leapt out of bed, and he too landed in what was now a soggy quagmire. "Fuck, what? Eh?" Rick looked under the bed and saw Sonja facing away from him. Still not noticing the handcuffs, he tried to pull her out, to save her, he thought.

"Fucking hell. What have you done? Son, nooooo". Rick was screaming hysterically.

Amber was screaming uncontrollably.

"Who's S... S.. Son, Sonja?" She blurted out.

"Shit, shit, shit, fuck. No please no…" Rick was hysterical, out of his mind. He couldn't take it all in. Maybe it was a bad trip, and he'd wake up in a minute, lying next to a warm Amber and it would have all been a bad dream. But no, the blood was still warm, still life in it. Maybe there's a chance, but Rick knew what she had done, and why. And now a loud knock on the door and an "Everything ok in there? I'm coming in."

The security guard and the receptionist had come to see what the commotion was, after neighbouring guests had complained, first about the music, and then the screaming. The sight that greeted them shook them to their core. Two naked bodies, covered in blood from the waist down, were sobbing, shaking, walking to and fro, in circles, holding their heads, pulling out their hair, manic, and moaning some incomprehensible gibberish. The security guard reeled back, arm out to try to stop the receptionist seeing inside, but it was too late, she immediately threw up into her hand, and ran out.

"Call the police Sandy, you ok to do that?"

"Yeah." she croaked.

Some of the guests came out, but the security guard stopped them. Sandy ran into an adjacent room and rang 999.

"Please go back to your rooms. NOW." He barked.

He turned back to the horrific sight inside room 505 and pleaded with the two hysterical, contorted, figures to calm down.

"What happened here? You been attacked?"

Then he noticed where the blood was coming from and saw Sonja lying motionless under the bed. Not really taking in the handcuffs. He wondered what the hell had just happened. Rick was pointing frantically towards the bed, while trying to console Amber, who was hitting him with her fists, and crying uncontrollably.

"Jesus, what's happened here?" He handed the pair dressing gowns from the back of the door, and said, "Put these on, cover yourselves up."

Then realizing this was going to be a crime scene, stepped back, trying not to get any blood on himself whatsoever. Nervous, in case they might attack him.

"I, I, I, don't know." Rick stammered between breaths. Saliva running from his mouth. "I, I, really don't know. We were in... in... bed, and found her underneath, it's my girlfriend, she's done this to punish me. Why? Why? Son, why? I am so sorry."

Amber passed out.

"Shit, help me, please." Rick asked.

"Sorry, not coming anywhere near you."

"Fuck....... Amber, wake up, wake up."

A knock on the door and Sandy peered in.

"What! No, no, what's happened?"

"Stay out Sandy, you don't want to see this."

"Christ, how much blood is in there? What's happened?" Sandy forced herself to look. "It's ok Frank, I have to see this."

"Sandy, really, I don't think you should.

"No, no, it's ok. What the hell happened here?"

"She, she," Rick stammered, "did this to me to get back at me. Shit. I didn't do anything, I mean it, I didn't do anything, I promise. Tell them Amber, tell them. Amber was frozen in shock, couldn't move, let alone speak.

"Ok, ok, let's all sit still for a minute. The police and an ambulance are on their way. They will be here soon." Frank was desperately trying to calm a horrific situation.

"Christ, is that your wife? That Mrs. Morelidge?" Sandy had just noticed Sonja, under the bed, "I let her in just a while ago."

"Wife? No, it's my girlfriend, she came to get her revenge." Rick said, looking at Amber, still frozen on her knees. Eyes looking nowhere and twitching occasionally. Sandy moved to see Amber. Frank put out his arm and stopped her.

"Don't go near them, the police will want to look at this."

Sandy ignored him, and carefully walked around the blood and held Amber close to her.

"Come with me", she said, "let's get you cleaned up."

"Sandy, don't. The police won't be happy, you really shouldn't."

"Come on Frank, she hasn't done anything. It's obvious what's happened. He's killed her, when she discovered them together."

"No, look at the handcuffs, look."

Sandy looked, and turned to Rick and said, "What have you done? You sick, perverted bastard."

Sandy backed away quickly and got Amber to the bathroom.

"Sandy, don't."

"Don't let him out of your sight Frank, and be careful, I'm here if he tries anything."

Some scuffling outside the door and a loud knock, two police officers entered, stopping dead in their tracks.

"Oh no." Said one of them. Quickly he moved into his emergency mode, every sinew, every nerve, every instinct, went on full alert, and he immediately weighed up the sight in front of him.

"What's happened here?" He asked Frank.

"Not sure. Look under the bed. I'm keeping out of it, my colleague is in the bathroom, helping a third party, we don't think she was involved in any of it. Haven't a clue how SHE got there." Pointing under the bed. "Don't know what's gone on here".

The police officer turned to his colleague and said to get the team down here, code 10 now.

Two paramedics arrived.

"Just wait there please." The police officer said.

"Actually, can you go to the bathroom, and see if they need help. I think one is staff, the other is something to do with this, I'm not sure."

"Will do." They both made their way to the bathroom, quickly taking in what was around them. They were used to seeing blood, but not this much. It was horrendous. One checked on Sonja and shook her head at her partner.

"Ok. Do you want to tell me what happened?"

"I fucking don't know what happened. I mean it. We were having sex in bed."

"Who?"

"Me and Amber, she's in the bathroom, Sonja," Rick pointed to her, "is my girlfriend and she must have sneaked in, and did this to herself, to get back at me."

"Handcuffed herself to the bed?"

"Yes. She does it all the time. It turns, turned, her on when we have sex. Strange, I know but she can do it. We did it a lot, oh Son, why? Why?"

"Ok, let's just wait for CID to arrive, they will take over, meanwhile just sit tight, let's not move anything here."

"That's what I said," added Frank. "Didn't want Sandy to take the other one in there, but she insisted."

"Don't worry, we'll soon get to the bottom of this." After a while another knock on the door.

"Hi mate. D.S.I. Lambert, and my boss Adrian."

"Hi."

"Hi."

"Ok what…. happened here?"

Rick explained what he knew. Frank explained what he knew. DSI Lambert ordered forensics immediately. Sandy and Amber came out of the bathroom.

"Who's this?" Asked Adrian.

"I'm Sandy, receptionist, this poor thing is Amber, sorry couldn't just leave her. I'm sure there is an explanation for all this." She said, looking pointedly at Rick. Rick shook his head, in his hands.

"I haven't done anything. I swear." He groaned, "tell them Amber please…"

Amber said nothing, still in shock.

"Where do you live honey?" Sandy asked her.

"The Somalian embassy. My father is the Attaché there."

"Oh shit." Said Adrian. "That's all we need."

"Can we get her home?" Sandy asked.

"Absolutely not, and I wish you hadn't cleaned her up. She may have been a part of this. They're both coming down to the station right now. Forensics will put suits on them to contain anything we can." Adrian looked under the bed, and carefully walked around the blood-stained carpet, examining Rick as he did. Forensics arrived; it was getting crowded in the room now.

"Can you swab him, fingernails too, take samples of what you need, then suit him and we'll get him out of here. Same with her, and we'll take them down to central. Call the Somalian Embassy and let them know where we're taking, Amber? Is it?"

"Yes." She whispered.

"Where we're taking Amber and can someone come down to help her."

God, what a mess thought Adrian. He walked around to the other side of the bed and noticed a thin trail of blood going under the curtain. Gently moving the curtain to the side, he found the Stanley knife.

"Over here." He beckoned one of the forensic team over.

"Can you photo that and bag it please and bring it with you, and what about her? She is handcuffed to all four posts; she couldn't possibly have done that herself could she? He's obviously tried to hide the knife here."

"Hmm, don't know." Said the paramedic.

"I do." Said Adrian.

"What's your full name son?"

"Richard Morelidge."

"And your girlfriend?"

"Sonja Jones"

"Richard Morelidge, I'm arresting you on the murder of Sonja Jones. You do not have to say anything, but what you do say will be taken down and used against you in a court of law.

"What?"